Advanced Praise f(

MW01047799

"Relationships are the agar-agar in the petri dish or life. Miller has provided one of the boldest and crucial books to help leaders and organizations in decades. Besides a magnificent shift in mindset, he provides many actions to avoid the quicksand often sucking us into low innovation, low engagement and low motivation."

Richard Boyatzis, PhD
Distinguished University Professor,
Case Western Reserve University
Co-author of the international best seller,
*Primal Leadership and the new The Science of Change:
Discovering Sustained, Desired Change from
Individuals to Organizations and Communities*

"In Real*ationship Driven Cultures*, Bryan Miller makes a compelling case for why relationships—not just strategy or innovation—are the foundation of thriving organizations. He explores how self-serving behaviors, division, and burnout erode workplace culture and offers a systems-based approach to fostering unity, self-worth, and resilience. By breaking down key workplace relationships—employee-employee, leader-employee, leader-leader, and company-employee— Miller provides a roadmap for building a truly connected culture.

This book is a must-read for leaders committed to creating workplaces where employees don't just work but truly belong."

Louis Carter
CEO and Founder Best Practice Institute and
Most Loved Workplace®

"This book is a masterclass in transforming workplace culture by prioritizing meaningful connections between people. If you're committed to building unity, self-worth, and resilience in your organization, this book is your roadmap."

Kary Oberbrunner
Wall Street Journal and *USA Today* Bestselling Author

"Rea*lationship Driven Cultures* invites readers to evaluate leadership through the lens of relationships. Backed by years of experience and research, Bryan highlights the behaviors that weaken connections and offers strategies to build stronger, healthier ones. In a time of divided views on ethical leadership, he makes a compelling case: relationships must come first even as we work to redefine the future of leadership."

Bob Welsh
Leverage HR

*REA*LATIONSHIP DRIVEN CULTURES

Foster Unity, Enrich Self-worth, and Build Resilience

*REAL*ATIONSHIP DRIVEN CULTURES

Foster Unity, Enrich Self-worth, and Build Resilience

BRYAN MILLER

ethos
collective

Published by Igniting Souls
PO Box 43, Powell, OH 43065
IgnitingSouls.com

LCCN: 2024920108
Paperback ISBN: 978-1-63680-386-9
Hardcover ISBN: 978-1-63680-387-6
e-book ISBN: 978-1-63680-388-3

Available in paperback, hardcover, e-book, and audiobook.

Any Internet addresses (websites, blogs, etc.) and telephone numbers printed in this book are offered as a resource. They are not intended in any way to be or imply an endorsement by Igniting Souls, nor does Igniting Souls vouch for the content of these sites and numbers for the life of this book.

Some names and identifying details may have been changed to protect the privacy of individuals.

DEDICATION

For my wife, Sherri, the woman who has shaped my life in ways too numerous to count. From the moment I met you, I knew I would marry you. Your love, patience, and unwavering belief in me have carried me through every challenge and fueled every pursuit. We have had many adventures and surprises and most likely will have more. Without you, none of this would be possible. I am forever grateful.

TABLE OF CONTENTS

PART 2: *REAL*ATIONSHIP-DRIVEN CULTURES

PART 3: OUTCOMES AND HOW TO GET THERE

TO THE READER

This book was written for you—leaders, business owners, and professionals who understand that relationships are at the heart of every great workplace.

You believe that culture should make work meaningful for yourself and others. Because you recognize that strong relationships are foundational, you prioritize them as a driving force behind engagement, retention, and performance. And most importantly, you're willing to do the work to make strong relationships a reality in your organization.

We live in a time where division, disconnection, devaluing of work, and burnout are on the rise. Yet, the most successful and fulfilling workplaces are those where people feel seen, valued, and connected. The power of relationships in the workplace is not just an idea; it's a necessity. Strong relationships fuel collaboration, trust, and innovation. They create cultures where people thrive.

I wrote this book because I believe relationships are not just important, they are essential. Over the years, I've seen companies struggle with disengagement, conflict, and burnout, and I've also witnessed what happens when leaders and teams commit to fostering strong, meaningful relationships. The difference is undeniable. When relationships are strong, trust grows, collaboration improves, and work becomes more than just a job; it becomes a shared purpose.

This book is more than a collection of ideas. It's an invitation to challenge the status quo, to lead with intention, and to create environments where relationships come first. I share a different way of thinking about workplace culture. Instead of quick fixes or solutions that address symptoms rather than the root cause, I offer a relationship-driven approach.

You'll explore the Three Foundational Beliefs, Four Key Organizational *Real*ationships, and Four Environmental Elements that create *Real*ationship-Driven Cultures. I share practical ways to apply them in your organization. As you read, I encourage you to reflect on your own experiences, apply the insights to your leadership, and take actionable steps toward fostering unity, enriching self-worth, and building resilience in your teams and organizations.

I am honored to share this journey with you. Thank you for believing in this message, for being a leader who prioritizes relationships, and for putting these ideas into action. Together, we can transform workplace cultures and, in doing so, create a lasting impact.

Let's get started.

INTRODUCTION

Why Relationships Matter More Than Ever

What if the biggest factor in your company's success isn't strategy, technology, or even talent—but relationships? Across industries, organizations struggle with division, self-serving behaviors, and disengaged employees. In fact, according to Elaine Houston, Gallup research shows that disconnected employees have a **37 percent higher absenteeism rate** and are **18 percent less productive** than their engaged counterparts.[1] Relationships aren't just a nice-to-have; they are the foundation of an organization's culture, performance, and resilience.

As I built a career in talent management, I was always searching for what would have the most impact on individual and organizational success. Because I did a lot of work with leaders and teams to improve performance, I was always curious about what brings people together and helps them focus on serving the greater good instead of only their own needs. This journey included learning about many great tools, assessments, and models to help bring employees together and improve relationships. I still use many of them today. However, I always felt like there was a more foundational and impactful answer.

My curiosity continued over the years. It drove me to explore new tools, models, and mindsets and improve my ability to use them to positively impact individuals, teams, and organizations. Then, one day, standing in my sunroom, it came to me. Relationships are the key. They are core and constant. No matter your organizational structure, team structure, industry, or company strategy, it takes relationships to get things done. Relationships have a large impact on culture and can influence it in either a positive or toxic way. Finally, being in a relationship is our deepest human purpose and has significant health implications.

The answer to improving relationships at work lies in creating cultures where strong, meaningful relationships thrive. I began integrating this philosophy into my work, refining my approach over time. What started as a way to improve my own impact in organizations evolved into a more comprehensive framework for transforming workplace relationships at scale.

As attitudes toward work have shifted, with division and burnout on the rise, the need for this work has only grown. Too many people see work as a mere transaction, valuing only the paycheck rather than the purpose. This perspective is uninspiring and flawed. When relationships are strong and meaningful, attitudes toward work shift, unity increases, and resilience develops.

If work relationships are strong and meaningful, attitudes toward work will shift, unity will increase, and resilience will develop. I committed to writing the book with the goal of impacting self-serving behaviors, lack of unity, and diminished self-worth to build resilience and fulfillment. For this to work, organizations will have to make a focused effort to create environments that bring employees together, provide them with purpose and meaning, and create a sense of accomplishment.

In this book, I will introduce and define how to build *Real*ationship-Driven Cultures, which are more holistic and proactive than using interventions or teambuilding activities to improve relationships. The need for help to work through issues will remain, but the need can be greatly reduced by a deeper understanding of how to nurture relationships and by building talent approaches that proactively provide structure and guidance for positive, strong relationships. This approach goes deeper than teamwork and common goals. It addresses how we interact, respond, and connect with each other.

I will outline how to strengthen relationships by creating an organizational environment and personal interaction approach that establishes a *Real*ationship-Driven Culture. The book will encourage you to view organizations as a collection of relationships and provide four key environmental elements to help relationships thrive and work toward organizational success. The goal is to Foster Unity and Enrich Self-worth that results in Resilience.

I built my talent management career during a transformational time in the history of organization development and change. The term "talent management" had just started being used about the same time I started working in organization development and learning. Over time, the term became more popular. It was not just a shift of semantics. The intent was to bring all work related to optimizing people in organizations together and make a much stronger connection to business outcomes.

I developed my career and impacted the use of talent management within the organizations I worked in. Always pushing innovation in people processes, I introduced first-time use of many talent processes, systems, and interventions in the organizations I worked for.

Throughout this time, many things have changed about how we find, manage, develop, and grow talent. I feel lucky to have been part of it and look forward to continuing my work to bring people together to make our organizations successful and a source of fulfillment for employees. Recently, many things have changed about how organizations operate and are viewed. As talent management and HR professionals, we need to morph our approach to respond to these changes. By focusing on relationships, we will truly get to the foundation of how our organizations operate: through the collective effort of people. Even the most automated industries need employees working together to be successful.

Knowing is good; doing pays the bills. My hope is that you will take action to improve and strengthen the relationships in your organization. For the most impact, an organizational approach is best. The more your systems and processes support the effort, the more traction you will get. The more employees actively support the approach, the more likely others will join.

Having said that, one person can have an impact. If you are not able to convince the organization to implement the approach, you can impact your team. Using the concepts will have a positive effect on those that you lead and interact with. You do not need a full organizational implementation to let the concepts impact your choices and how you interact and treat others. I encourage you to put the learning into practice to build workplaces that employees enjoy participating in and find value in contributing to.

My approach to talent management and, ultimately, to building *Real*ationship-Driven Cultures was profoundly shaped by my time at Case Western Reserve University. Earning my degree in Positive Organizational Development and Change shifted my perspective on how organizations grow, evolve, and thrive. Rather than focusing on what's broken, I learned to ask, *What do we want to become?* Instead of working to eliminate dysfunction, I embraced the power of building toward something better. This philosophy is the foundation of my work, moving organizations toward Unity, Self-worth, and Resilience rather than merely correcting issues of division, burnout, and self-serving behaviors.

A positive approach doesn't ignore challenges, it redefines how we address them. Too often, organizations try to categorize problems, segmenting people into groups, labels, or silos that only reinforce division. But real change happens when we build commonality, not separation. When we focus on shared goals rather than competing agendas, we create cultures where relationships thrive. This book is built on that premise. *Real*ationship-Driven Culture isn't about fixing what's wrong; it's about fostering what's right.

PART 1

THE CASE FOR RELATIONSHIPS

Relationships shape every aspect of life. They can be deeply fulfilling or incredibly painful. Whether between two people or within larger groups, relationships influence our experiences in work, school, family life, and beyond. This book focuses on work relationships because they are essential to both individual and organizational success.

Throughout my career, both in corporate leadership and independent consulting, I have witnessed workplace relationships of all kinds, from toxic and dysfunctional to deeply enriching and productive. Some relationships are built on trust, shared purpose, and mutual respect, while others exist primarily for personal gain.

In some cases, individuals and teams form relationships strategically, aligning themselves with those who can advance their own interests. This self-serving approach leads to division, distrust, and, ultimately, burnout. In contrast, the strongest work relationships are rooted in genuine care, shared goals, and a commitment to something greater than personal success. When people find unity in their work, build meaningful connections, and feel a sense of purpose, work relationships become a source of strength rather than stress. The result is greater resilience both individually and collectively.

This section explores the three major issues that weaken workplace relationships—self-serving behaviors, division, and burnout. It lays out the challenges of relationships and why they are ultimately the key to a thriving workplace.

CHAPTER 1

THREE ORGANIZATIONAL ISSUES: SELF-SERVING BEHAVIORS, DIVISION, AND BURNOUT

The best work relationships have unity beyond working as a team. Employees have deeper connections, and they care about each other. Relationships also benefit from doing impactful work together, valuing each other, and achieving organizational success. Through unity, meaning, and purpose, work and relationships are less stressful and become a source of enjoyment. The result is more resilience.

When relationships are not positive and strong, it causes three critical people issues: an increase in self-serving behaviors, division between employees, and eventually burnout from a toxic environment. My effort to solve the problems caused by self-serving behaviors led me to explore options to overcome them. I concluded that healthy relationships would have the most impact. As I continued to advance my thinking regarding how to bring relationships to the forefront in organizations, other workplace issues were increasing in severity and frequency. Employees were becoming more disconnected from each other. Multiple cultural factors drove this disconnect. Many organizations have become more focused on political issues than serving customers.

In some cases, our workplaces have become political hotbeds, losing focus on the purpose of our work. The workplace environment has become more hostile, divisive, and self-serving, which leads to a disconnect regarding the value of work. In fact, self-serving took on a whole new element. Instead of self-serving workplace behaviors solely focused on advancing one's career, self-serving became a way to serve specific political agendas. Employees pressured companies to serve their political beliefs, which led to increased division.

With these three issues on the rise, I decided to expand, refine, and organize my original concept of focusing on cultural work with relationships as the foundation. I decided to design everything on the premise that relationships are our deepest purpose and that organizations are a collection of relationships. I increased my writing as a way to advance my thinking and understanding of the impact of focusing on relationships.

Self-Serving

I have worked with many teams at all levels throughout the world. Self-serving behaviors are the single most detrimental behavior in organizations. The behavior often goes unchecked, especially if the individual can create the perception of getting good results. Typically, the self-serving individual can accomplish a lengthy list of tasks but leave a path of destruction along the way.

Sometimes, the behavior is not addressed because leaders do not want to risk upsetting the individual for fear of interrupting what seems to be good results. What is not considered is that the productivity of the company overall is most important. One individual cannot contribute enough to make a company successful. Employees who engage in self-serving behaviors are generally good at making the right connections and controlling the narrative, so the destruction is masked, and the blame ends with everyone else.

Although important, it is not just people's feelings that get hurt. Overall productivity falls for several reasons. Employees will spend time venting and checking in with others to understand their reactions to the self-serving behavior. There may also be time spent trying to figure out how to respond to less than optimal solutions, and most likely missed important details because the self-server has not bothered to listen to others and seek the best solution. They simply want to complete a task or project and move to the next one, even if quality suffers.

Self-serving employees have little time for their peers, direct reports, and stakeholders unless they need something from them to advance their cause, which, of course, is their own success. In one extreme example, a leader required his direct reports to get agreement from him to have a meeting before going to his admin to set up a meeting. This resulted in blocking direct reports' access to him. He spent very little time in his office, didn't respond to emails, and did not take phone calls. Additionally, he did not have regularly scheduled one-on-one meetings. Employees could be seen hanging out near his office for long periods of time, hoping to catch him just to get permission to set up a meeting to discuss issues or get a decision from him.

On top of that, he liked to be involved in most decisions, even the lowest-level decisions. As you can imagine, the work product was slow, and the team was extremely frustrated. He did this to free up his time to manage up and make connections that would secure his next promotion. He was successful with this strategy for some time. Eventually, it caught up with him, and he was let go.

Another misuse of relationships happens when teams build superficially strong relationships with each other at the expense of relationships outside the team. The focus is on supporting each other at all costs. Challenging each other and accepting negative feedback from outside the group is extremely resisted. By taking a self-preservation mindset, the team and its individuals do not grow or produce work that is well thought out or vetted in the organization. If a team does not get beyond unquestioning support for each other, they will always be at risk of focusing more on their own needs at the cost of the organization's needs.

In extreme examples, individuals and teams become toxic. They become so focused on their own needs and self-protection that they engage in destructive and unethical behavior. They believe their success at all costs equals organizational success, so the ends justify the means. Lying becomes the norm. Blaming others for failures and taking credit for the accomplishments of others is a way of raising their credibility and reducing the credibility of others. They view the reduction of the credibility and performance of those around them as a means to build their credibility and increase their chances of being promoted. You would think this behavior would be easily detected and overcome. In my experience, it is not.

There are several barriers to detecting and overcoming these toxic behaviors. Many victims of blame-shifting are reluctant to speak out. Most organizations today value teamwork yet do a poor job of defining what it means to be a good team member. The definition of a good team member can inaccurately be interpreted as a need to get along with others all the time at all costs. They may also be conflict-avoidant, hesitant to embarrass others, or afraid of being seen as attention-seeking or credit-grabbing. These mindsets create a situation that escalates. As the blame shifter gets away with small infractions, the infractions become more egregious. A similar thing happens with lying. Small lies become bigger lies.

While working with a research company, I witnessed a typical example of how self-serving behaviors can create the appearance of good results. In reality, it is many hours of wasted time and unnecessary frustration. The company did not have good internal audit processes, which resulted in findings from external audits. An experienced auditor was hired to create and implement internal audit processes.

The organization's goal was to set up internal audits to improve the success of the external audits. The lead auditor's primary personal goal was to set up internal audits as quickly as possible without concern for accuracy or benefit to improving the company. In an effort to be seen as a hero who saved the company, he created an audit process by himself with no input from any of the functions or time spent learning about the work. He did not seek to understand the functions, their processes, or how they contribute to the company's overall success.

He scheduled "collaboration" meetings with each function after he created the audits and presented the internal audit processes as "just trying to help get things started." He assured everyone that his list of audit items and measures were editable to meet the needs of the function. It quickly became apparent that they were not editable. Even the simplest questions and suggestions were met with extreme resistance from the new lead auditor.

The lead auditor controlled the narrative by frequently reporting to his manager and the senior leadership team. He convinced them that the functions were resistant to change and was trying to prevent internal audits from happening. The functions had to decide how to respond. They could just accept the audit as is or try to push for adjustments. None of the functions were against creating good internal audits. They did not want to be seen as resistant, but accepting the audits as is was not good for the business.

One simple example of the problems with the audit came from the talent acquisition function. One of the lead auditor's measures was to have the same number of job requisitions across all recruiters. As you can imagine, this measure would create extreme inefficiencies and actually be less fair to the recruiters. Recruiting an entry-level position with routine tasks is extremely different from recruiting a PhD research scientist in a very specialized field. This simple logical explanation was met with resistance from the lead auditor and an unwillingness to discuss it.

In the end, the function decided to push back, and the measurement was changed. However, many hours were wasted internally by the function deciding what to do and how to go about it. Additional hours were wasted meeting with the auditor, the auditor's manager, and other leadership to gain support to review and adjust measures like this one and others. The time spent countering the belief that the functions were just being resistant was a total waste of resources. Self-serving behaviors were reinforced because of the amount of time they were allowed to continue and the praise the auditor received along the way and at the end of the project.

There were many examples like this one that created waste. In some cases, the functions decided not to push back and just accepted the list of audit items. This choice avoided the time spent on negotiating and gaining support to make the audit meaningful. However, the functions were then left to chase metrics that were not valuable and, in some cases, detrimental to the business.

There were no consequences for the behavior. The project was perceived as successful even though many hours were spent above what it should have taken. In some cases, the quality of the internal audits was subpar. It measured things that were not important. Additionally, internal audit compliance was disconnected from external compliance requirements, which caused poor business decisions to follow compliance with the internal audit. The auditor was viewed as overcoming resistance that simply was not there. However, since he had built artificially connected relationships with the right people, his story became the "believed" story. This simple yet real example highlights the importance of using relationships in a way that increases productivity and cooperation toward the greater good.

Unfortunately, examples of self-serving behavior are easy to find. In recent history, companies like Enron, Volkswagen, Uber, and Wells Fargo fell victim to self-serving behaviors. When leaders and employees take focus off the greater good, bad things happen. Self-serving behaviors tend to happen over time. A selfish decision. A small rule broken. A slight ethical slip. Then, it grows from there.

Wells Fargo, one of the largest and most respected banks in the United States, was once known for its conservative management style and strong ethical values. However, in the early 2010s, the bank embarked on an aggressive strategy to cross-sell products to its existing customers.[2] The leadership, including CEO John Stumpf and other senior executives, set ambitious sales targets for employees, pushing them to sell multiple products such as checking accounts, credit cards, and insurance products to individual customers. It started innocently as a way to improve company performance.

As these aggressive sales goals became harder to meet, Wells Fargo executives developed a culture that prioritized sales above all else, even if it meant bending or breaking the rules. The bank's management put intense pressure on employees to meet unattainable quotas, often threatening job security if these goals were not met. This led to widespread unethical behavior.

Employees, under pressure to meet sales targets, began opening millions of unauthorized bank accounts and credit card accounts in customers' names without their knowledge or consent. Estimates suggest that over 3.5 million fraudulent accounts were created between 2011 and 2016.

Some employees forged signatures and altered customer contact information to prevent customers from noticing the unauthorized accounts. Others enrolled customers in services they did not request, such as overdraft protection, online banking, or bill pay, all to meet the daily or weekly targets set by their managers.

The bank's leadership set sales goals that were often impossible to achieve through legitimate means. Under the slogan "Eight is Great," employees were told to sell at least eight products per customer. These unattainable targets led to a toxic culture in which employees felt they had no choice but to engage in unethical practices.

Employees who tried to report unethical behavior were often retaliated against. Many whistleblowers faced disciplinary action, were fired, or were otherwise penalized, further discouraging others from speaking out.

Under intense public scrutiny and pressure, John Stumpf resigned in 2016. In 2020, the U.S. government fined him $17.5 million and banned him from the banking industry. His reputation, once built on trust and ethical leadership, was severely tarnished, and he faced significant financial penalties.

Carrie Tolstedt, the head of Community Banking who directly oversaw the division responsible for the fraudulent activities, was also forced to resign. The government fined her $25 million and accused her of playing a significant role in the scandal. Tolstedt's actions were seen as prioritizing personal financial gains over ethical conduct, leading to her downfall.

Over 5,300 employees were fired for their involvement in the scandal. Many claimed they were simply following orders and trying to meet unrealistic sales goals. The scandal left many employees without jobs and with damaged professional reputations, even though the bank's aggressive sales culture had pressured them into the behavior.

Millions of Wells Fargo customers were directly impacted by the scandal. Many found themselves paying unexpected fees for accounts they never authorized or were subject to credit score damage due to unauthorized credit card openings. The fraudulent accounts led to financial hardship, damaged credit, and a loss of trust in the banking system.

The scandal led to a sharp decline in Wells Fargo's stock price, wiping out billions of dollars in shareholder value. Many investors, including pension funds and individual shareholders, suffered significant financial losses.

Wells Fargo faced substantial fines and penalties from multiple regulatory bodies, including a $185 million fine in 2016 from the Consumer Financial Protection Bureau, the Office of the Comptroller of the Currency, and the City and County of Los Angeles. The total cost of settlements, legal fees, and compensations has exceeded $3 billion. The scandal caused a massive loss of trust in Wells Fargo. The bank's reputation as a reliable and ethical institution was severely damaged. Customers closed their accounts, and new customer growth slowed significantly. Wells Fargo's brand value plummeted, impacting its market position and ability to attract new customers.

In addition to financial penalties, the Federal Reserve took the unprecedented step of imposing a cap on Wells Fargo's growth, barring the bank from increasing its total assets beyond the level they were at in December 2017 until it improved its governance and risk management practices. This growth cap has limited the bank's ability to expand its business operations, affecting long-term profitability.

The scandal led to a complete overhaul of the bank's leadership. The new CEO, Charles Scharf, was brought in to lead a cultural transformation and restore the bank's reputation. However, the process has been slow and ongoing, with the bank still facing skepticism from regulators, customers, and investors.

The Wells Fargo scandal serves as a stark reminder of the dangers of self-serving behavior at all organizational levels. It illustrates how short-term personal gains can lead to long-term damage for individuals, employees, customers, and the entire organization. By prioritizing ethical behavior, transparent leadership, and realistic goal setting, organizations can avoid such pitfalls and foster a culture of trust, integrity, and accountability.

Division

Division in the workplace is on the rise.

The increase in workplace division has multiple root causes, including the previously mentioned politicization of the work environment. The lack of focus on relationships and self-serving behaviors are also the main contributors to division.

A 2021 report by Gallup revealed that 43 percent of US employees said they experience some form of conflict at work. Divisive issues like political beliefs, social justice, and the COVID-19 pandemic have exacerbated tensions among coworkers, and social media has further amplified workplace conflicts.

Politics

For nearly all controversial political issues, the country is more or less divided equally. When senior leadership chooses a side on controversial political issues, it automatically divides employees. Employees will feel compelled to pick and defend their position even at work. While senior leadership is responsible for the overall direction and high-level decisions, these decisions seem outside their purview. Employees are the company. They are not an asset to be managed. Picking a side diverts attention, focus, and energy from the company's purpose of serving customers. The customer suffers.

I believe business can and should benefit society. Our organizations should be held accountable for seeking profits responsibly. It is good to expect them to go beyond a do-no-harm philosophy. They should make the communities where they are better and even reach beyond that as profits allow. Building parks, supporting the creation of better housing, feeding the hungry, and helping fight disease are just a few ways to make the world a better place for everyone. These causes are an excellent way to use the success of a company to serve communities and the world.

Relationships

A second root cause is that there is not enough focus on relationships. Through processes and tools, Organization Development has increasingly helped employees interact more positively with each other. For example, DiSC®, 360 feedback tools, behavioral assessments, and team development stages help us understand ourselves and others better. The tools help us identify and leverage patterns of human behavior.

There are many more examples of tools and processes beyond what I have listed. They are helpful, and I have seen them produce great results. We should continue to use these tools since they do have a positive impact on relationships. I will lay out in detail ways to take our thinking and approach to improving organizational relationships to a deeper level.

Self-Serving Behaviors

A final root cause is self-serving behaviors. Of course, they result in division. Positive relationships are give and take. There should not be a scorecard or tally sheet that is tracked to create total equality. Yet, each person in the relationship must contribute and feel valued. We show our love for others through sacrifice. The sacrifice can be monetary, time, or actions, whether large or small. The sacrifice is more appreciated if there is no expectation of reciprocation.

Self-serving employees do not generally sacrifice for others' success and certainly do not do so without expecting something in return. Under these circumstances, it is difficult to connect, if not impossible, resulting in division.

When our relationships are united and purposeful, we are free to accomplish the work in the best way possible. Our minds are free to brainstorm, explore options and debate solutions. We are not preoccupied with how different we are from those we work with. The differences are likely to come out and even be leveraged. It will just be more natural and freer from tension. These relationships cause less stress, are more productive, and benefit everyone.

Burnout

When employees are disconnected from each other and their work, it is easy to become disillusioned with work. Studies show that money is a short-term motivator. If employees view their job as merely a paycheck, it is hard to overcome the stressors that come with work and working with others. Without purpose and meaning, work seems like it is not worth the effort. Going to work becomes a meaningless chore focused only on earning money for survival.

Work-life balance has been a topic of discussion for a long time, but concerns have recently increased. In some cases, readjusting work-life balance was both needed and good. However, it seems that we have over-adjusted. Work-life balance can be difficult to get right. There are no specific criteria that help us determine what good balance looks like. If we emphasize work too much, our personal life suffers. If we under-emphasize work, we may not have the resources needed to have a fulfilling life, and we miss an opportunity to add value and gain self-worth through our work and service to others. Our ability to impact society diminishes, and we decrease our social networks if we just go through the motions in our work lives.

It is hard to be resilient when we do not feel united with our coworkers. We don't get the benefit of feeling like we are in it together. The potential for connection and fulfilling our deepest purpose of being in a relationship is there but not realized. The division deepens, and the stress of working with others increases.

Additionally, it is hard to be resilient when we do not feel valued. If we are not involved in running the business in a meaningful way, our self-worth decreases. A work environment lacking a service culture makes it hard to realize and recognize the contributions of every employee. The select few who focus on promoting themselves dominate the opportunity to contribute and receive the bulk of the recognition. In this environment, many employees' self-worth is diminished. It is hard to avoid burnout when our potential is not realized and we are not recognized for our contributions. The benefits of working hard are increasingly unknown or forgotten.

When we contribute at work, we are part of something bigger and create positive social networks with our coworkers. Humans are wired to be in relationships. Social networks at work can provide beneficial relationships that are both fulfilling and healthy. Working hard provides a source of satisfaction. It feels good to do your best, which contributes to a positive mindset.

As we overcome obstacles, we gain a sense of achievement and build confidence. This prepares us to attack other life challenges and setbacks positively, reducing stress and increasing resiliency. Further, our sense of gratitude increases, and we learn to enjoy the journey as we overcome struggles. Time is one resource that steadily passes no matter what. You cannot save it or store it. Working in a meaningful way ensures you use your time wisely and increases your sense of accomplishment.

No matter what you do for work, you are contributing to society. Someone wants or needs the product or services your company provides. Therefore, others benefit from your contributions. Many times, employees underestimate the value they provide. Not everyone is a lifesaving doctor or a million-dollar deal maker. Yet someone somewhere benefits from what you do, or you would not be paid to do it.

It reminds me of an old story.

A woman was walking down a sidewalk next to a construction site. There were three workers spread out along her path. She approached the first one and asked the worker, "What are you doing?" The worker replied, "Laying brick." She asked the second worker the same question. The worker replied, "Building a wall." She asked the third worker the same question. The worker replied, "I am building a cathedral where people will worship, gather to enjoy each other, and some will get married here."

All three were doing the same work and working on the same building. Yet, they had three different perspectives regarding their work. I encourage everyone to think about their work in terms of the benefits they are providing to others. Be the third bricklayer!

Another example of understanding the value of work came from a story told by a family member. He told me about a neighbor with a young son working at an elderly nursing home. The neighbor's young son faces a lot of his own issues, yet he loves working and helping others. When his dad told him he didn't have to work anymore if he didn't want to, he replied, "But what will the people do?" He truly understood the value of his work. It was not about him; it was about the service he provided to others.

Company cultures have played a large role in creating the aversion to working hard and having a commitment to company success. The largest negative impact on company culture is self-serving behaviors. Leaders and employees who are largely focused on gaining benefits for themselves. They seek results and accolades for their own benefit at the cost of others. Creating a *Real*ationship-Driven Culture can diminish self-serving behaviors, encourage strong relationships, and create a company culture where hard work is not crippling. It is invigorating and allows everyone to thrive.

Positively Affecting Organizational Behaviors

As I explored the newer issues of division, burnout, and self-serving behaviors, I contemplated how to positively impact all three. I realized that I already had the answer: relationships. If relationships are positive and strong, it will affect all three issues. I concluded that the approach must Foster Unity, Enrich Self-worth, and Build Resilience. Through Unity, employees feel a deep connection to others and are concerned for others' success. This connection creates a willingness to build, maintain, and prioritize relationships. When self-worth is high, employees are more likely to cheer for the success of others. Self-worth also creates meaning and purpose, increasing a desire to work. Unity and Self-worth work together to create a positive attitude, a hopeful outlook, and a sense of value. The result is Resilience. By systematically and purposefully encouraging strong, positive relationships focused on the greater good, we can create cultures where everyone thrives.

I have increasingly recognized the importance of relationships. They impact our quality of life, our ability to get things done, and, ultimately, our happiness. When our relationships thrive, we thrive. At work, relationships impact engagement, employee experience, and productivity. When relationships are healthy and positively focused, the employee experience is good, and productivity goes up. When relationships struggle, so do employees' health and their performance.

My focus on relationships is different than networking or teamwork. They are both important and useful, but my work is designed to go deeper by creating Unity, Self-worth, and Resilience through deep connections and strong relationships. Broadly speaking, networking is about creating and leveraging connections for mutual benefit. Teamwork is about having a common work goal and creating synergy around accomplishing that goal. The focus on relationships is deeper. It is more than providing mutual benefit on specific topics. Building strong relationships is about creating purpose for relationships that go beyond team or work goals.

CHAPTER 2

SELF-SERVING LEADERSHIP CHARACTERISTICS: HOW TO RECOGNIZE IT IN YOURSELF AND OTHERS

Self-serving leaders damage relationships, erode trust, and disrupt an organization's ability to succeed. They focus on their own interests at the expense of the teams and people they lead, often leaving long-term consequences and a negative impact on culture. Recognizing these tendencies in ourselves and others is critical to building an environment where such behaviors are not tolerated or rewarded. This chapter explores the traits of self-serving leaders, how to identify them, and how to overcome them.

Self-Serving Behaviors

- **Focus on managing up:** They spend an inordinate amount of time promoting themselves to their manager and others higher in the organization. It comes at the expense of leading their team.

- **Divide and conquer:** When dealing with issues within the team, they gather information from team members separately. Solutions are determined by what benefits their career.

- **Short-term focus:** These individuals look for solutions that most benefit their career in the short term, not the truth or the best overall solutions.

- **Take credit for others' work:** They often claim successes as their own while avoiding accountability for failures.

- **Prioritize personal image over team success:** The focus is on looking good to upper management rather than addressing underlying issues or fostering team growth.

- **Hoard information:** These people withhold critical information to maintain control or gain a perceived advantage over others.

- **Manipulate relationships for personal gain:** They are masters at using charm or influence to build alliances that benefit themselves rather than the organization.

- **Avoid investing in others' development:** It's rare for these people to mentor or invest in the growth of their team because they see no direct benefit to their career.

- **Deflect blame:** They are quick to point fingers at others when things go wrong rather than taking responsibility.
- **Exploit positional authority:** They use their role to intimidate or dominate rather than inspire and empower.
- **Overemphasize personal success metrics:** Their focus is exclusively on metrics or achievements that reflect well on them, even if they are detrimental to broader organizational goals.
- **Undermine peers:** They sabotage or belittle colleagues to appear more competent or indispensable.
- **Exhibit inconsistent values:** They likely speak about the organization's mission and values but act in ways that contradict them when it serves their interests.

This list helps us recognize, understand, and deal with behaviors that are counterproductive to *Real*ationship-Driven Cultures and organizational success. The caution is to not be too judgmental or jump to conclusions. Sometimes, these behaviors are subtle, and we may misinterpret what is happening. We may not have all the relevant information, which could lead to misinterpretation. It is best to look for patterns, seek additional information, and address situations starting with curiosity.

Part 1: Recognizing Self-Serving Leadership in Yourself

Leadership starts with self-awareness. Even the best leaders can fall into self-serving habits when under stress, pursuing career goals, or navigating challenging dynamics.

Recognizing these tendencies early helps us course-correct and build stronger, more meaningful relationships.

Conduct an Honest Self-Reflection

The first step is an honest inventory of your own behaviors. Reflect on these questions:

- Do I focus more on impressing my superiors than supporting my team?
- Have I avoided taking responsibility for mistakes while claiming credit for successes?
- Do I view peers as competition rather than partners in achieving goals?

Write down your thoughts and look for patterns. Self-serving tendencies often reveal themselves in how we prioritize actions and measure success.

Listen to Feedback from Others

Your team and peers may recognize behaviors you haven't noticed in yourself. Pay close attention to feedback:

- Have team members expressed frustration about a lack of support or transparency?
- Do colleagues suggest that your priorities are misaligned with the team's goals?

If feedback isn't forthcoming, consider asking for it through a structured process, such as anonymous surveys or 360-degree reviews. Be open, reflective, and willing to hear difficult feedback.

Examine Your Motivations

One of the simplest ways to uncover self-serving behavior is to examine your decision-making process. Ask yourself:

- Why am I making this decision?
- Am I choosing the path that benefits my team or just myself?
- Am I prioritizing short-term recognition over long-term impact?

Through reflection, you may uncover misaligned priorities, which will help you make better, more balanced choices.

Part 2: Recognizing Self-Serving Leadership in Others

Identifying self-serving leadership in others requires careful observation and an understanding of their impact on the team. Often, their behaviors are subtle but consistently harmful.

Observe Patterns of Behavior

Self-serving leaders exhibit signs that, when observed over time, reveal their true priorities:

- Do they focus on managing up while neglecting their team?

- Do they avoid accountability, deflecting blame to others?
- Are they more concerned with crafting and protecting their image than solving problems?

Look for recurring behaviors rather than isolated incidents, as patterns often tell the full story.

Analyze Their Impact on Team Dynamics

Self-serving leaders often leave behind fractured teams. Pay attention to how the team functions:

- Are team members divided, with favoritism or competition replacing collaboration?
- Do employees feel undervalued, unsupported, or disengaged?
- Is there tension or frustration that seems to originate from the leader's actions?

Teams led by self-serving individuals frequently experience low morale and high turnover, clear indicators of deeper issues.

Watch for Discrepancies Between Words and Actions

Actions speak louder than words. Self-serving leaders may talk about teamwork and values while acting in ways that contradict them. Ask yourself:

- Do their decisions reflect what they claim to prioritize?

- Are they fostering unity or creating divisions?
- Do they follow through on commitments or back-track when it's inconvenient?

A lack of alignment between words and actions strongly indicates self-serving motives.

Pay Attention to Communication Style

The way a leader communicates often reveals their intentions. Watch for signs of self-serving behavior:

- Do they dominate conversations and dismiss others' ideas?
- Is their communication more focused on self-promotion than team outcomes?
- Do they avoid difficult conversations or shift blame when confronted?

Effective leaders prioritize clarity and collaboration; self-serving leaders prioritize control and personal gain.

Part 3: Addressing Self-Serving Leadership

Recognizing self-serving behavior is only the first step. The real work begins when we address it. Whether the behaviors are in ourselves or others, we must take deliberate action to create a healthier, more *Real*ationship-Driven Culture.

Call Out Behaviors (Respectfully)

When you notice self-serving tendencies, address them directly but constructively. Frame the conversation as an opportunity for growth. For example:

- Share specific examples of how the behavior impacts the team or organization.
- Focus on solutions rather than assigning blame.

Approaching the conversation with respect increases the likelihood of a positive outcome. You must remember that your personal and reporting relationship with the self-serving leader impacts your ability to address the behaviors. If you have a close relationship with trust, you are more likely to get a positive result. If there is tension in the relationship, it will be harder to have a positive outcome. If you report to the self-serving leader, it may be difficult to have a conversation regarding their behavior. Some leaders are very open to feedback, and some are not.

As a peer to the self-serving leader, the outcome of addressing the behavior rests on the strength of the relationship. The direct leader of the self-serving leader likely has the best chance to impact the negative behavior.

Shifting Away from Self-Serving

Recognizing and addressing self-serving leadership is critical to building a culture that values relationships, trust, and collaboration. Whether these behaviors exist in ourselves or others, awareness is the first step toward change. By identifying these traits and taking deliberate action, we can create environments where self-serving behaviors are discouraged and relationships are strengthened.

Throughout the rest of the book, we will explore how to build a culture that inherently discourages self-serving tendencies by focusing on systems, mindsets, and practices that empower leaders to serve their teams and organizations first, thus reducing the need to address self-serving behaviors individually. Together, we can create *Real*ationship-Driven Cultures that inspire everyone to succeed.

CHAPTER 3

WHY RELATIONSHIPS ARE HARD, YET REWARDING AND WORTH IT

Relationships can be difficult for multiple reasons. Understanding how and why relationships can be hard helps us to navigate them better and increases our chances of building strong, lasting relationships. Sometimes, people retreat away from relationships in the face of difficulty. As people reduce their relationships, their loneliness increases, resulting in reduced purpose and increasing the health implications outlined earlier.

We are designed for survival. It is how our brains and bodies are wired. This, of course, is good. It is why we are still here. However, sometimes, it prevents us from having good interactions and relationships with others. There are four specific areas I am referring to. First is fight or flight, which most people are familiar with. When we feel threatened, we go into self-preservation mode. The second is holding on to negative thoughts longer than positive thoughts. Third is confirmation bias, where we create a hypothesis and more naturally look for things to confirm our belief rather than things that dispute it. Finally, associative learning helps us react efficiently and speedily but can create inaccurate thinking.

Fight or Flight

When I ask who has heard about fight or flight in leadership development workshops, most people have heard of this. Many people also understand that it causes them to behave in undesired ways. In a disagreement, they either say nothing or attack the other person. A large number of people have no idea why it happens. We must first understand what is happening if we are going to avoid being a victim of fight or flight. So, I always explain briefly before we move on to ways to combat it.

In very basic terms, we have three parts of our brain—the right and left brain, which processes logic, language, and abstract thinking, and a smaller part of our brain at the stem, sometimes called the reptilian brain. Its job is to process information extremely fast. However, it does this at the expense of thoughtful analysis and logical reaction. When we are in a life-threatening situation, this is very beneficial.

We take in all information and stimuli through the brainstem, which processes the information within hundredths of milliseconds. The data is processed to detect threats and elicit a response—fight or flight. The reptilian brain has been key to human survival. When our ancient ancestors were hunting, they would encounter many different animals. They had to be able to make quick decisions when they came across an animal. There wasn't time to evaluate the situation. They couldn't try to determine how many teeth it had, how much it weighed, or other relevant information. They had to quickly answer the question, "Am I going to eat today, or is that animal going to eat today?"

When the brainstem suspects a threat, it responds quickly. Blood is directed to major muscle groups like arms and legs and not as much to our right and left brain. This prepares the body to stay and fight or flee to safety. Either choice will benefit from the higher performance of our major muscles. At the same time, adrenaline is surged to increase our ability to fight or flee.

We do not face as many threats as our ancient ancestors. We are not likely to run across a saber-toothed tiger. This brain function can still serve us well in emergency situations. Fight or flight becomes a liability when we do not accurately assess what is and is not life-threatening. For example, if I give a presentation and someone criticizes it afterward, I may interpret that as a threat and have a strong negative response. It may not feel good. It may even hurt my feelings and ego. However, I am not likely to sustain any injuries from it. My negative response could prevent me from learning and damage the relationship. If the person intended to help me perform better and I attack them, the relationship will be damaged.

To overcome this natural response, we can do several things. Most of us received advice from our parents when we were young. They told us to count to ten before responding when we got mad. Whether they knew it or not, this is good advice based on biology. By counting, we provide time to process the situation more fully, and we engage our logical left brain. Even though counting is a simple task, we must use our left brain to do it.

We can remind ourselves that few situations are truly life-threatening. Someone sharing information, discussing a difficult topic, or even insulting you is not life-threatening. You will most likely get a better result if you have a measured response. Being curious, even in tense situations, can also help us control our response rather than our response controlling us. Being curious gives us time to process the information more completely and increases our understanding of their position. There will be plenty of time for a strong response if it is warranted. It is better to have a calculated response than a knee-jerk reaction. Relationships benefit from curiosity in several ways. Reduced defensiveness creates more collaborative interactions. Curiosity increases learning. When we learn more about others, it creates stronger connections because we understand them better, and they feel understood.

Negativity Bias

Negativity bias describes our tendency to "attend to, learn from, and use negative information far more than positive information."[3] We can think of it as an asymmetry in how we process negative and positive occurrences to understand our world, one in which "negative events elicit more rapid and more prominent responses than non-negative events."[4]

It is thought to be an adaptive evolutionary function.[5][6][7] Our ancient ancestors faced more daily threats than we do, so negativity bias played a critical role in survival. Although we have fewer threats on a daily basis, we still need to remember what a threat is to us so we can survive. It is still necessary for human survival, even though it may not play as big a role as it once did. So, we can be thankful that our brain has evolved to operate that way while having the ability to adapt to ensure it doesn't impede our ability to have good relationships.

Even without research, we know this to be true. Have you ever had something bad happen and just could not forget it or let it go? Most of us have. We replay it over and over in our minds even though we tell ourselves that we are going to move on. Think about the last insult you got. Now, think about the last compliment you got. Which one is more memorable? For which do you remember more details and have a stronger emotional response to even now? If you are like most of us, you answered the insult.

In a Harvard Business Review article titled "The Ideal Praise-to-Criticism Ratio", Jack Zenger and Joseph Folkman discussed the importance of overcoming our negative bias.[8] The study analyzed the effectiveness of 60 strategic business unit leadership teams by examining their financial performance, customer satisfaction ratings, and 360-degree feedback. The findings revealed that the highest-performing teams had an average ratio of 5.6 positive comments for every negative one, while medium-performing teams had a ratio of 1.9 to 1, and low-performing teams had a ratio of 0.36 to 1, indicating nearly three negative comments for every positive one. This suggests that a higher frequency of positive feedback is associated with better team performance.

When I first learned about this concept, I did a little personal experiment. At the end of the day, I asked myself whether it was a good or bad day. I forced myself to answer quickly without replaying the day in my mind. Then, I would think back and list all the positive and negative things that happened that day. I would have more positive than negative most days. However, even on days that were overwhelmingly positive, I had classified the day as negative. I started forcing myself to replay the day before answering the question, "How was your day?"

Knowing that we have a stronger and longer-lasting reaction to negative events, we can make sure we do not overemphasize the negative in our interactions with others. Unchecked, we can overreact to negative interactions with others. We remember other negative reactions more than positive reactions, leading us to evaluate the situation more negatively than it actually is.

By understanding negativity bias, we can intentionally assess our interactions with others more holistically. A purposeful, balanced assessment of the person, situation, and overall relationship can elicit a more accurate response to your specific situation. Just knowing we are more likely to respond more negatively than appropriate may provide the pause needed to have a balanced response that is more likely to preserve the relationship.

Confirmation Bias

Definition: "The tendency to gather evidence that confirms preexisting expectations, typically by emphasizing or pursuing supporting evidence while dismissing or failing to seek contradictory evidence."[9]

One of the early demonstrations of confirmation bias appeared in an experiment by Peter Watson in which the subjects were to find the experimenter's rule for sequencing numbers.[10] Its results showed that the subjects chose responses that supported their hypotheses while rejecting contradictory evidence.

As it relates to survival, we must sometimes make very quick decisions. In modern times, confirmation bias continues to play a role in how we process information, especially in high-pressure or high-stress situations where quick decisions are necessary. Today, we have an exponentially larger amount of information to process. Without grouping and categorizing the information, it would be impossible to make quick decisions. As the research suggests, though, these decisions may not be based on facts.

Not all confirmation biases are negative. Some positive reasons for confirmation bias are maintaining our confidence in our beliefs and values, protecting our self-esteem, and giving us a sense of certainty and security. Consider a firefighter responding to a building engulfed in flames. Over the years, the firefighter has learned that smoke rising rapidly in a specific way often indicates a flashover—a sudden and intense burst of flames that can be deadly. The firefighter's experience has created a pattern in her mind that certain types of smoke mean danger.

While fighting a fire, the firefighter sees smoke that matches this pattern. Despite not having complete information about the exact conditions inside, she quickly makes the decision to evacuate her team from the building. The firefighter is acting on confirmation bias—believing that the smoke behavior confirms the threat of a flashover because it aligns with what she has seen in the past.

In this situation, confirmation bias helps the firefighter process complex information rapidly, potentially saving lives. While it may lead to the occasional false alarm (e.g., evacuating when there is no flashover), the bias supports survival by encouraging quick action in situations where hesitation could be fatal. The bias toward expecting danger based on past experiences can prevent catastrophe, even if it sacrifices some accuracy for speed and safety.

In this modern example, confirmation bias aids decision-making by prioritizing immediate safety over exhaustive analysis, showing how it remains a valuable, albeit imperfect, tool for survival in urgent situations.

Unfortunately, confirmation bias can also be detrimental to good decision-making. Since our natural reaction is to react quickly using incomplete information, we fall victim to not analyzing the situation more fully even when time allows, and decision quality is preferred over immediate reaction. Additionally, if we do not force ourselves to look for information that disaffirms our initial beliefs, we lose an opportunity to learn and have more fully developed opinions. Developing a list of pros and cons is a good way to overcome confirmation bias.

This can negatively impact relationships when we create an initial opinion about someone and only look for things that support that first impression. This mistake prevents us from having fully developed opinions of and attitudes toward the people we meet.

Association Learning

Association learning is a normal way our brains function. It makes it easier to process information and can speed up decision-making. The unconscious part of the brain finds patterns, makes connections, and categorizes things. This can be both good and bad.

As related to survival, categorization is good. It allows us to make quick decisions. Take big cats, for instance. If I am on a safari and a big cat is approaching, I can quickly decide what to do. I do not need to process if it is a lion or tiger, male or female, or any other factors. I just need to process that big cats are faster, stronger, and more aggressive than humans and that I need to protect myself somehow. Categorization also helps us more efficiently learn and understand the world around us. For example, birds are a category. We do not have to learn everything about each bird. We know generally that birds fly, do not have bladders, and eat seeds. This helps process the large amount of information we are faced with.

On the negative side, decision quality and completeness can suffer. If we think of people as only fitting into a category that we may have unconsciously put them in, we are stereotyping. It prevents us from interacting with them as individuals. Some common categories we place people in are nationality, political view, personality type, and others. Julian Baggini tells us in *The Ego Trick*: "Human beings think in terms of stereotypes for good reasons. Without mental shortcuts, we simply couldn't get by. There is just too much information to process, and we often have to be quite crude as to how we filter it."

In our relationships, this categorization can get in our way. We may "categorize" people we meet based on a few or even one characteristic. Of course, this is bad. Although people may have some similarities to others in a given group, they likely have many differences too. Also, most people fit into more than one category. For example, a few categories I fit into include male, married, and business owner, to name a few. Obviously, I am not the same as everyone in each of those groups.

People are complex and different in an almost infinite number of ways. We must remind ourselves of how different people can be and stay curious about getting to know them better. A great way to build relationships is to be truly interested in learning more about the people you meet. Although our work relationships are less likely to be as intimate and involved as our personal ones, learning more about our coworkers is still a great idea to strengthen our work relationships.

Personality

We all have different personalities, which can differ in many ways. Even with 8 billion people on the planet, no two are the same. The ways in which we are different are extensive. The differences can get in the way if we let them divide us. At times, we do not understand that not everyone thinks like us, responds like us, and approaches things the way we do. When people view others as not behaving properly because they don't do things the same way, it causes conflict.

Because of our tendency to assume negative intentions, those differences can become a wedge between us and others. When we assign negative intentions to others, we tend to avoid addressing the issue, which leaves the conflict unresolved. For example, when a project is assigned, some people want to jump in and get started. Other people like to gather data and information. If negative intentions are assigned, it is a difficult conversation to work out the balance between getting the project done and gathering information. The correct balance of getting done versus gathering data differs for every project and is impacted by many factors. Therefore, it takes some navigation.

The person wanting to gather more data could see the person pushing to completion as uncaring regarding the quality of the project. The person wanting to push to completion may see the data person as lazy. These are difficult conversations to have. If we understand that personalities differ and we have a strong relationship, we are more likely to assign positive intent. In this example, the positive intents are getting the project done on time and having the right amount of data and information to deliver a quality project.

There are assessments that help employees understand and deal with these differences. One of my favorites is DiSC. The tool I use can be applied in unique ways, increasing its usefulness. Additionally, by applying the systems and processes outlined in upcoming chapters in this book, organizations can build strong relationships and cultures where working out these differences is easier and more appreciated.

External Environment (Life Situations)

Unfortunately, several environmental forces are working against us as we try to build *Real*ationships. The most common external environmental barriers include organization politics, world culture that focuses on self, lack of formal relationship skills education, dealing with life's situations, and a lack of an approach to relationships.

Every organization has politics. Some have more than others, and some are more negative than others. Harold Lasswell, a prominent political scientist, defined politics as "who gets what, when, how." This definition emphasizes the distribution of resources and decision-making processes within groups. This foundational work by Harold Lasswell provides a succinct and influential definition of politics, focusing on the processes by which power and resources are distributed within societies. Lasswell's approach underscores the practical and relational aspects of political decision-making. There will always be competition within an organization for limited resources, such as budget and headcount, to name a few. Politics become especially troublesome when they are used for personal gain. Employees understand if the navigation and decisions regarding resources are focused on the greater good. If navigation and decisions are based on someone's personal gain, employees instinctively know it is bad, creating resentment.

Self-serving politics in organizations has a significantly negative impact on workplace relationships, contributing to stress, reduced engagement, and decreased job satisfaction among employees.

Forbes discusses the impact of organizational politics on trust and collaboration in the article "How a New CEO Can Repair a Culture Dominated by Office Politics." The article emphasizes that when office politics become pervasive, they can lead to decreased employee engagement and retention, as well as erode trust and collaboration within teams. It suggests that leaders should actively work to mitigate negative political behaviors to foster a more positive and productive organizational culture.

This impact can be quantified. One meta-analysis examining the relationship between perceptions of organizational politics and stress found a mean corrected correlation of 0.45, indicating a strong association between political behavior and increased stress levels in the workplace. This heightened stress often translates into lower job satisfaction and increased turnover intentions, ultimately weakening employee commitment to the organization.[11]

Using organizational politics for personal gain is self-serving. Self-serving behaviors have one of the highest negative impacts on relationships. They create division and resentment among employees, which can lead to decreased excitement and effort toward the organization. Left uncorrected, these self-serving behaviors become the norm, and you end up with a toxic culture. Employees either check out mentally or physically.

It's difficult to escape the influence of self-serving behaviors. Modern times have people increasingly focusing on themselves. We are told in commercials to put ourselves first. Society tells us to look out for number one. Win at all costs is a common mantra. Self-help and self-care are everywhere. Many people try to "find" themselves. Safe spaces have become the norm. Trigger warnings are common. The pursuit of avoiding any and all pain has people retreating into themselves.

By overly focusing on self-protection and hiding from adversity, we do not learn how to face difficulty with courage and a sense of accomplishment in overcoming obstacles. We should encourage each other to overcome difficulties, not retreat or hide from them. Of course, if we can avoid them, we should. However, once life's obstacles, struggles, and stressors emerge, we should deal with them with strength and the attitude of a conqueror.

Most people don't know how to do this. Employees often lack the basic skills to manage relationships. For the most part, schools do not do much to formally teach relationship skills. They provide guidance, feedback, and discipline as issues arise. At home, children can learn about relationships, but there, too, it is most likely guidance, feedback, and discipline as issues arise instead of proactive, structured learning.

Relationship skills training can go a long way to improve the strength of relationships. Some organizations provide this type of training, while others do not. Some organizations offer it to all employees, and some only to higher-level employees. There is a lot more we can to provide everyone with a work environment that promotes strong relationships, healthy cultures, and job satisfaction.

Interpersonal skills like good communication, conflict resolution, and emotional intelligence help build strong relationships.

- **Good communication skills** help create understanding, set the tone for our relationships, and allow interactions to be positive even in difficult situations.

- **Conflict resolution** is critical to strong relationships. We are not likely to agree with everything our coworkers say, think, and do. Being able to resolve differences and conflicts is necessary. One barrier to being better at conflict resolution is the misconception that conflict is bad and should be eliminated. Conflict is not bad. Mishandling conflict is bad. Conflict is a key element of learning and innovation. Getting comfortable and proactively dealing with conflict makes it productive.

- **Emotional intelligence (EI)** has been linked closely to success. EI is our ability to recognize and regulate our own emotions as well as the ability to recognize and respond to the emotions of others. Humans all respond with emotion. It is just how humans are wired. Even the most non-emotional person you can think of processes information emotionally first. Therefore, emotion plays a role in our behavior. EI allows us to use our emotions in a positive and productive way.

Life has an impact on our response to others. Most people have complex lives with a lot of things going on at any given time. If we or the person we are interacting with are dealing with negativity in our lives, we may not react to or interact with others the way we would like. Sometimes, we have both positive and negative things happening simultaneously. It makes it difficult to understand how we should feel. We teeter between being happy for the positive and sad for the negative, which creates an emotional roller coaster. This emotional confusion can result in us being frustrated or upset quickly.

These external environmental barriers have the potential to put stress on our relationships. By having formal organizational systems, processes, and learning in place, we can minimize the negative impact of these external environmental obstacles. A *Real*ationship-Driven Culture enhances the quality and strength of our relationships.

By learning to navigate our relationships, we can make them a source of fulfillment and enjoyment. When you understand the common stressors, you can avoid the traps that infect our relationships needlessly.

CHAPTER 4

WHY RELATIONSHIPS ARE THE ANSWER: WE ARE RELATIONAL

We are designed to be in relationships with others. It is our deepest human purpose. Even if we have convinced ourselves that we don't need others, something will always be missing when we don't connect. Being in a relationship fulfills our deepest human needs. Our work relationships will usually not be as intimate as other relationships, yet they hold unique value. Work relationships are an opportunity to contribute to the success of others and the overall company. When companies succeed, they provide jobs, contribute products and services, and, most times, make some philanthropic contributions. This activity contributes to the economy and overall success of society.

The evidence for relationships being our core purpose and that we are designed to be in relationships is overwhelming and undeniable. Two main sources make the case for the importance of relationships. First, my experience tells me we are designed to be in relationships. Second, health data shows the extreme importance of relationships.

My Experience

During my talent management career, I have worked with teams to improve their performance. I use several methods and assessments to determine the root cause. There are typically a variety of issues negatively impacting team performance. Although I have seen many issues while doing this work, they tend to fall into a few categories, including relationships, processes, policies, structures, mindsets, or skills issues.

Almost always, relationships are either a contributing factor or the issue. Relationship issues are always part of the equation because, with good relationships, those other issues would have been resolved. When poor relationships are present, employees tend to fixate on the relationship issues. Relationship issues are a source of high stress. The result is reduced time and focus on attacking issues that will increase efficiency and productivity in the right way and with the right vigor. Poor relationships can also hinder direct, challenging counter-opinions. Employees hesitate to challenge each other when relationships are not strong. They fear the reaction and potential negative conflict.

Another key observation includes the impact of good relationships on the need for relationship improvement processes and tools. As one simple example, in the organizational and leadership development work I do, I teach employees how to give and receive feedback. I have a process and guidelines that help reduce defensiveness and increase acceptance of feedback.

I have seen these tools increase the use and effectiveness of one of the best organizational learning tools: feedback. However, the stronger the relationship and the more united the employees are, the less these tools are necessary. When we have strong relationships, we have higher levels of trust and are more likely to assume good intentions. That trust makes us much more open to feedback and less sensitive to how it is given.

Health Data

Health data tells us that loneliness plays a major role in our lives. Loneliness does not have a positive impact. What is loneliness? It is a lack of relationships. The absence of human connection. The Oxford English Dictionary describes loneliness as "sadness because one has no friends or company." In the context of this definition, the word company is used to mean "being with others."

Interestingly, "company" can mean a business and being with others. The original meaning of the word was to be with others. Over time, it came to mean "a number of persons united to perform or carry out anything jointly."[12] It eventually came to mean a commercial business. It seems that the transition of the word, which took place in the late 14th century, implies a humanistic value in doing business together.

> Today's Oxford dictionary definitions are:
>
> 1. a commercial business:
>   "a shipping company" · "the Ford Motor Company" · "a company director"
> 2. the fact or condition of being with another or others, especially in a way that provides friendship and enjoyment:
>   "I could do with some company."

As companies became larger, they focused more on profits and stockholders. We lost some of the focus on the human aspect. In recent years, companies are trying to bring back the human aspect. We have more to do and need a shift in how we refocus on the human aspect. For example, many companies proudly say employees are their "biggest asset." They say this with good intentions, but it highlights the need for a mindset shift. Although companies are trying to highlight the value of their employees, they inadvertently diminish the fact that employees "are" the company.

Many organizations today recognize the need to be more human-centered, yet some of our well-intended efforts have backfired. In trying to create workplaces where people feel seen and valued, we have often focused too much on what makes us different rather than what unites us. Initiatives meant to foster inclusion can sometimes unintentionally reinforce separation. Efforts to personalize work experiences can, at times, create silos that erode teamwork and trust. The result? More division, more stress, and a workplace culture that feels fractured rather than connected.

This isn't to say that acknowledging differences is wrong. It is essential to understand people's unique experiences, perspectives, and needs. But when we build systems that overemphasize categories, we risk losing sight of the most fundamental truth: we are all human. Work should not be a place where we are defined by our labels but where we are united by our shared purpose. If we want to create truly human workplaces, we must rethink how we approach relationships in organizations. Instead of focusing on distinctions that separate, we need to focus on connections that bring us together. We must shift toward a culture built on unity, self-worth, service, connection, and shared purpose. If we do this, we can truly transform the way we work.

Human beings are inherently social creatures, designed to thrive in the company of others. Our need for connection is deeply rooted in our biology, and when this need is unmet, it can lead to significant health consequences. Loneliness, a state of perceived social isolation, has been linked to a myriad of physical and mental health issues.[13]

Physically, loneliness has been associated with increased mortality and a higher risk of cardiovascular, metabolic, and neurological disorders. Research indicates that individuals experiencing chronic loneliness are more susceptible to heart disease, stroke, and dementia. A systematic review of multiple studies found strong evidence linking social isolation to poorer health outcomes, particularly in cardiovascular and neurological health.[14] These findings underscore the importance of strong relationships in maintaining long-term well-being.

The immune system is also adversely affected by loneliness. Chronic social isolation has been shown to increase inflammation and reduce antiviral responses, making individuals more vulnerable to infections and disease. Research on leukocyte transcriptome dynamics found that people who experience prolonged loneliness exhibit an increased expression of pro-inflammatory genes, which can contribute to chronic diseases and a weakened immune response.[15] This biological response demonstrates how deeply interconnected our social environment is with our physical health.

Mentally, the repercussions of loneliness are equally concerning. Persistent loneliness has been found to significantly increase the risk of psychiatric disorders such as depression, alcohol abuse, sleep disturbances, personality disorders, and even Alzheimer's disease. A growing body of research highlights that individuals with fewer social connections are at a much higher risk of cognitive decline and mental health issues.[16] This evidence suggests that fostering meaningful relationships is not just about emotional well-being. It is a crucial factor in maintaining mental resilience.

Furthermore, loneliness contributes to higher stress levels, disrupts sleep patterns, and can create a feedback loop that exacerbates mental health challenges. Studies have shown that individuals who feel socially isolated have elevated levels of cortisol, the stress hormone, which negatively impacts both physical and mental health.[17] As stress levels rise, it becomes even harder to engage in social interactions, further deepening the cycle of isolation.

The evidence is clear that strong, meaningful relationships are not just beneficial but essential for both physical and mental health. Our design as social beings necessitates connection, and without it, we risk significant health challenges. By building and maintaining relationships, we not only enrich our lives but also build resilience against the adverse effects of loneliness.

Business Benefits

Creating work cultures where positive, strong relationships thrive has business benefits. In workplaces, relationships foster belonging, which is tied to employee engagement and productivity. According to the National Business Research Institute, high-trust work environments increase productivity by 50 percent, improve employee retention, and reduce burnout.[18]

The Pew Research Center found that employees who report having good relationships with their coworkers are much more likely to be satisfied with their jobs overall—even in situations where they may be dissatisfied with other aspects, like pay.[19]

Innovation is critical to organizational success. To keep pace with the competition and ever-changing business environment, organizations need to be adaptable, change-ready, and great at problem-solving. Workplaces that encourage strong relational bonds see higher levels of creativity and collaboration. A study from MIT examines how teams of scientists and engineers utilize their social networks to gather new ideas and feedback.[20] The study demonstrates that both within-team networks and members' extended networks significantly influence the teams' problem-solving abilities. Notably, the strongest ties within these networks have a substantial effect on performance, highlighting the importance of social connections in fostering innovation.

This study underscores the critical role that social networks and interpersonal relationships play in enhancing creative problem-solving and innovation within teams.

The term "soft skills" originated in the 1960s within the U.S. military to differentiate between skills requiring machinery or specific tools (hard skills) and interpersonal skills (soft skills) used for tasks like leading or managing teams. Over time, this terminology expanded to the corporate world, where "soft skills" came to mean people skills. Unfortunately, the name "soft" implies that these skills are easier to learn or less essential than hard skills, which has led to a persistent underestimation of their value.

MIT Sloan School of Management researchers conducted a study with Shahi Exports in India.[21] This study evaluates the impact of a 12-month soft skills training program. Findings revealed that trained workers were 20 percent more productive than their untrained counterparts. The program yielded a 258 percent return on investment for the firm within eight months post-training, primarily due to increased productivity. Additionally, the training enhanced workers' extraversion and communication skills, leading to technical skill upgrades.

When organizations invest in building great cultures, they become a force for good and create a thriving business. Culture will happen. It is a question of whether it happens to you or because of you. As you can see from the data, relationships have both personal and business impacts. The case in which relationships are inextricably connected to business is strong. Investing in *Real*ationship-Driven Cultures provides both humanistic and business benefits.

What If We Do Nothing? Who Is Affected and How

While healthy relationships can significantly enhance your life, they can also cause high levels of stress when things go wrong. One APA survey highlighted that poor relationships with colleagues or supervisors can lead to chronic stress.[22] Chronic stress from negative workplace relationships can significantly impact both physical and emotional health.

Workers experiencing ongoing interpersonal conflicts may develop issues such as anxiety, depression, sleep disturbances, and a weakened immune system.

Chronic stress can severely harm physical health, causing symptoms like headaches, stomachaches, and exhaustion. Over time, prolonged stress may even contribute to severe health conditions such as cardiovascular disease and hypertension.

This data points out the importance of strengthening our work relationships. *Real*ationship-Driven Cultures get everyone involved in creating an environment where strong relationships focused on serving thrive. When we make serving relationships "the way we do things around here," it gets easier for employees to behave in serving ways. If we don't improve the culture in our organizations, they will continue to be a source of stress instead of a source of satisfaction.

A recent study by Ricoh USA underscores the importance of fulfillment at work.[23] Employees ranked their overall fulfillment at 6.89 out of 10, with 51 percent reporting that they feel less fulfilled compared to five years ago. Perhaps even more troubling is that only 21 percent of employees feel completely fulfilled through their work, and nearly half (47 percent) say they feel more disconnected from their colleagues than they did five years ago. These numbers paint a stark picture of what happens when organizational cultures fail to prioritize the relationships that fuel engagement, connection, and purpose.

The consequences of neglecting workplace culture extend far beyond the walls of our organizations. The Ricoh study revealed that 82 percent of workers say their sense of fulfillment at work directly impacts their happiness at home. This means that when employees feel disconnected or unfulfilled at work, it spills over into their personal lives, perpetuating a cycle of dissatisfaction. Meanwhile, 91 percent of workers believe that culture is the key to fulfillment at work, and 84 percent say their sense of fulfillment is a deciding factor in whether they stay with their current company. These statistics highlight the direct link between workplace relationships, employee retention, and overall well-being.

Organizations must recognize that creating a culture where relationships thrive is not just a nice-to-have, it is a strategic imperative. Building a Relationship-Driven Culture is the smartest investment any company can make, not only to address the rising tide of employee dissatisfaction but also to ensure their business has a lasting, positive impact on the lives of their employees. Purpose-driven work, a focus on work/life balance, a growth-oriented culture, and an environment that minimizes unnecessary friction are all priorities workers ranked as critical to their fulfillment and are the byproducts of strong workplace relationships. Failing to address these needs will inevitably result in higher turnover, decreased engagement, and missed opportunities to unlock the full potential of the workforce.

The further we move away from understanding the value of work, the harder it will be to reconnect. Like most issues, the longer they move in a direction, the more difficult it is to convince people to think differently. It will take more than a different narrative to turn the trend around. We must fundamentally change the way we look at organizations and how we impact organizational environments to build strong cultures where people want to come to work and find value and fulfillment. We must build company cultures where everyone thrives.

Work should be a source of provision, a sense of accomplishment, and a method of adding value to society. If the value of work is diminished, we will experience a loss of productivity, a reduced sense of personal accomplishment, and, eventually, a stark decline in society's overall prosperity. Nurturing a working environment that encourages positive relationships is the key to turning this around.

Our organizations play a valuable role in society and our personal lives. They provide the products and services we all need to survive and thrive and increase our enjoyment of life. Our work lives hold the possibility to provide the fulfillment of our deepest purpose, which is relationships, as well as increase our sense of self-worth through accomplishment. Lack of enthusiastic participation in work life will likely decrease innovation and competitiveness of the organizations that do not create great work cultures.

*Real*ationship-Driven Cultures provide the systems, processes, and mindsets to help organizations build great work cultures where employees want to work and are fulfilled through their work. In the words of the late great Vince Lombardi "Build for your team a feeling of oneness, of dependence upon one another and the strength to be derived by unity." Creating a culture where teams are united, depend on each other, and draw strength from each other provides physical and mental health benefits that fuel organization success.

PART 2

REALATIONSHIP-DRIVEN CULTURES

A Systems Approach

Relationship (noun)
re•la•tion•ship (ri•lā•shən•ship)

1. The state of being related or interrelated
2. The relation connecting or binding participants in a relationship

> *Real*ationship (noun)
> Re•al•a•tion•ship (Rēal•a•shǝn•ship)
>
> 1. Next-level relationships, enhanced by three foundational beliefs and four environmental elements to foster unity, enrich self-worth, and build resilience
> 2. Builds connection to each other and the work

Focus on Relationships

Organizations, in their essence, are not merely collections of systems, processes, or structures; they are, more fundamentally, a collection of human connections and relationships. The quality and strength of these connections and relationships are the foundation for building organizational success. It is within this context that we begin our exploration of the transformative power of *Real*ationship-Driven Cultures.

The main objectives of *Real*ationship-Driven Cultures are to make our relationships stronger, more meaningful, more productive, and more satisfying. Focusing company culture on relationships benefits the individual and the company. Strong relationships create workplaces that people want to be part of. The employee experience is positive and a source of satisfaction and fulfillment. When energized and passionate, people are productive and more capable of overcoming challenges.

*Real*ationship-Driven Culture is a systems approach. The idea is to overwhelm the organizational environment with relationship-promoting people systems. The intention is to impact mindsets and behaviors to bring people together, make them feel valued, and get them engaged in their work.

This section starts with a discussion on culture. It covers the system which includes Three Foundational Beliefs, Four Key Organizational *Real*ationships, and Four Environmental Elements that create Three Outcomes. Details, obstacles, and implementation strategies are shared for each aspect of *Real*ationship-Driven Cultures.

Our deepest purpose and greatest strength are relationships
Relationships are core and constant in organization life
Organizations are a collection relationships

Employee to Employee — Create connections between employees
Leader to Employee — Leader commits to success of employees
Leader to Leader — Leaders work toward organization success
Company to Employee — Systems to engage employees in
running the business

MINDSETS
How we treat each other

INVOLVEMENT
How we work together

PURPOSE
Why we work together

SERVICE
How we win together

UNITY
In it together

SELF-WORTH
Feel valued by adding value

RESILIENCE
Effort is worth it

CHAPTER 5

UNDERSTANDING CULTURE: AN OVERVIEW

How Culture Is Created

Culture is the result of a collection of decisions and choices to solve problems, overcome barriers, and navigate life. Whatever is successful tends to become the culture. Culture can be both strong or weak and good or bad. Strong cultures tend to have consistent choices, approaches, and expectations. In weak cultures, there is more variation in how people approach things. Good cultures are rooted in healthy behaviors, while bad cultures promote unhealthy behaviors.

As a simple work example, let's look at decision-making in group meetings. As employees navigate the decision process, talking loudly and abrasively to shut others down when expressing their opinions is something that works to "win" the decision. The more this happens, the more employees approach it this way. Over time, it becomes the culture. If this approach is reasonably consistent across the organization, the culture becomes strong and negative. It is strong in that it happens often and in different settings. It is negative because abrasive cultures are stressful and rarely yield the best results.

Two basic human characteristics help drive the creation of culture. They are deeply rooted in who we are, making them difficult to change. That is why it is important to guide your organizational culture early and often.

The first human characteristic is our desire to fit in with the group. Most people have some desire to fit in. Conformity theory has shown this to be true. In two studies I will cover later, Milgram and Asch use the theory to encourage negative behavior. Milgram demonstrated that people would dangerously shock others to go along with the researcher and his research. Asch convinced people to give a wrong answer to fit in with the group. We suggest using the theory for good. By creating an environment where strong, healthy relationships are prioritized, we can convince others to behave similarly. Unity, self-worth, connection, and fulfillment thrive when culture has a foundation of relationships.

The second human characteristic that drives culture is deeply held values. I am sharing the three studies below to show that our values impact our behaviors at work. Because they are deeply held, they can be difficult to change and we may even not fully make the connection between our values and the decisions and choices we make.

Personal Values and Innovative Behavior

A study by Purc and Laguna explored the relationship between employees' personal values and their innovative behavior.[24] The researchers found that values emphasizing openness to change and self-enhancement positively correlated with innovative actions, while values centered on conservation and self-transcendence had a negative correlation. This suggests that personal beliefs significantly impact how employees approach tasks and contribute to organizational innovation.

Values at Work: The Impact of Personal Values in Organizations

A comprehensive review by Arieli, Sagiv, and Roccas examined how personal values shape various workplace outcomes.[25] The study concluded that employees' core beliefs influence their job performance, satisfaction, and interactions with colleagues. For instance, individuals who prioritize benevolence are more likely to engage in cooperative behaviors, while those who value achievement may focus on personal success.

Personal Values and Their Impact on the Opinion Leadership of Managers and Employees

Research published in 2024 analyzed how personal values affect the opinion leadership of both managers and employees.[26] The findings suggest that deeply held beliefs play a crucial role in shaping how individuals influence and guide others within an organization, impacting decision-making processes and leadership effectiveness.

These studies collectively highlight that employees' deeply held personal beliefs significantly influence their workplace behavior, interactions, and overall performance, often surpassing the impact of formal organizational values or missions. That is why *Real*ationship-Driven Cultures start with Three Foundational Beliefs, which will be covered in detail in later chapters.

In the previous example, the desire to be successful impacts the approach. Winning feels really good. Even the least competitive person you know likes to win. Similarly, we like to feel successful and that we are having an impact. This, of course, drives us to do what works. If yelling and demeaning others is successful, at a minimum, we are at least tempted to do it. At the maximum, we feel compelled or forced to be antagonistic. Another way to think about winning is power. The desire for power is strong in humans and similar to the concept of winning. Although levels vary, we all seek some level of power and typically view gaining power as winning.

Culture is difficult but not impossible to change. Since culture is built over time and is based on what works, it takes some concentrated effort to change it. We can change the culture if we are intentional and willing to do the work. In my culture work, I start with the foundation of strong, positive relationships that serve the greater good because our need to be in relationships is deeper than our values.

I have done a lot of work related to change in organizations including culture transformation, continuous improvement, behavior change, and technology implementations. I developed a framework to help me think about how to gain adoption of change. I use an iceberg to describe my Three Levels of Desire. The three levels include, starting at the top of the iceberg, "Have to", "Willing To", and "Want To." The iceberg is a good representation because the top is most visible yet does less to impact the direction or movement of the iceberg. It is what is below the water line, Willing To and Want To, that has the most impact. Of course, the more we move people to Want To adopt change, the more successful the change will be.

All three levels are important. It can be tempting to only focus on getting employees to want to implement a change. The problem is that the Want To level is harder to achieve. The strategies to influence employees to Want To level are harder to find, take more time to convince, and are more individualized. In change, momentum is critical. If we only rely on reaching the Want To level, we will likely lose momentum and not successfully implement change.

Culture transformation is especially difficult and requires leveraging all three levels. The Have To level is achieved through policies, procedures, and work rules. Typically, these are driven by consequences. Positive consequences reinforce compliance. Negative consequences address non-compliance. Consequences can be both natural or imposed. An example of a natural consequence is a team that frequently misses deadlines due to poor communication and lack of collaboration. Over time, their reputation for reliability diminishes, and other departments bypass them for critical projects, reducing their influence and opportunities.

An example of an imposed consequence is when leadership implements a new policy requiring teams to submit weekly progress reports and attend mandatory project check-ins to ensure better communication and accountability. Teams that fail to comply are excluded from high-visibility initiatives until improvement is demonstrated.

The Willing To level is achieved through communication, training, and influence. It is important to share why the change is important and how it ties to company objectives. As you get quick wins and convince some employees to adopt the change, more employees will buy in, remember Conformity Theory. Good communication and training builds skills and confidence that employees can be successful in the new way of doing things, which is something most of them will be worried about.

The third and deepest level is Want To. Reaching this level is more difficult but yields fuller adoption of the change. The best way to achieve this level of buy-in is to connect the change to employees' deeply held beliefs, values, and personal benefit. Different departments and functions may be impacted differently in the same change, making it more difficult to influence this level of desire. Add in the fact that individuals are unique and it increases the difficulty level.

Although difficult, achieving the Want To level is attainable. Good change management is a good investment and is known to increase adoption. I won't go into the details of good change management here. I could write an entire book on it.

A *Real*ationship-Driven Culture is a change-friendly environment. It creates an environment that emphasizes good relationships, which bring employees together to openly discuss change and work together to help each other and the company be successful. Serving the greater good provides the right balance of company and personal needs. Involvement helps employees feel like the change is happening with them and because of them, as opposed to the change happening to them. Purpose creates the desire to focus on the customer and know the importance of the work they are doing. When employees understand the importance of their work, they naturally want to improve it. Mindsets help employees preserve relationships through the conflict that arises during change while challenging each other appropriately.

Importance of Culture

Culture remains a crucial factor in today's organizations. Although it varies by sector, culture plays a significant role in job satisfaction. In a 2023 study found on zippa.com, they broke out the percentage of impact culture played in job satisfaction.

Private	**42%**
Nonprofit	**65%**
Government	**67%**
Self-Employed	**62%**

No matter what sector you are in, culture is important to your employees. Dissatisfied employees have a negative impact on company results. Job satisfaction stats frequently exclude the reality that the problem of disgruntled employees also has significant financial implications. Businesses that ignore employee satisfaction cost the United States as much as $450–550 billion annually, leading to an increase in turnover, lower employee productivity, employment drives, and a general lack of effort on their part.[27]

CHAPTER 6

THREE FOUNDATIONAL BELIEFS

---

3 FOUNDATIONAL BELIEFS ────────────────●

1. Our deepest purpose and greatest strength are relationships
2. Relationships are core and constant in organizational life
3. Organizations are a collection of relationships

---

*Real*ationship-Driven Cultures start with Three Foundational Beliefs, which set the stage for incorporating the rest of the system. If we truly believe in the importance of relationships, we want to focus on them. The desire to focus on and prioritize relationships is the foundation of building a *Real*ationship-Driven Culture.

When we understand how important relationships are, it is only natural that we start viewing organizations as a collection of relationships. Defining organizational *Rela*tionships helps us understand them and work to optimize them. Each of the *Rela*tionships is unique, has different interactions, and serves a distinctive purpose for the organization's success.

Our Deepest Purpose and Greatest Strength Is Relationships

The Claim

We are designed to be in relationships with others. It is our deepest purpose. Life is more enjoyable when we share it with others. During times of struggle, we can lean on others. Sometimes, they have great advice, and sometimes, they just listen. Either way, we typically feel better.

At work, our relationships help us feel part of something bigger than ourselves. Additionally, work products typically benefit from the diversity of thought that occurs with healthy work relationships. Work relationships usually differ from other relationships but add another dimension to our deepest purpose. Of course, there are times when our work relationships turn into friendships.

Support for the Claim

Gable and Gosnell explored the concept that humans possess distinct reflexive brain networks dedicated to social cognition.[28] Their research indicated that close interpersonal relationships are beneficial to health, as they enhance certain biological systems that may offer protection against the negative effects of stress. Specifically, they found that social interactions can trigger the release of oxytocin, a hormone associated with trust and the motivation to assist others in professional settings.

Robin Dunbar's research in 1998 proposed that the experience of social pain, such as feelings of isolation in the workplace, activates the same regions of the brain as physical pain.[29] This overlap suggests that social and physical pain share common neural pathways, highlighting the profound impact of social connections on human well-being.

The Centers for Disease Control and Prevention (CDC) has highlighted the significant health risks associated with social isolation and loneliness.[30] According to the CDC, social isolation can increase the risk of dementia by 50 percent, heart disease by 29 percent, and stroke by 32 percent. Additionally, loneliness is linked to higher rates of anxiety, depression, and suicide. The economic impact is substantial, with loneliness costing the U.S. economy an estimated $406 billion annually.

A Harvard Study of Adult Development, commonly known as the Grant Study, is one of the longest-running studies on human happiness and health.[31] Initiated in 1938, it has followed 268 Harvard sophomores over several decades to identify the factors contributing to a fulfilling life. The study's findings indicate that close relationships, more than wealth or fame, are key to happiness and health throughout life. These relationships protect individuals from life's challenges, help delay mental and physical decline, and are better predictors of long and happy lives than social class, IQ, or even genetics.

A 2010 meta-analysis led by Julianne Holt-Lunstad examined the impact of social relationships on mortality risk.[32] Analyzing data from 148 studies encompassing over 308,000 participants, the research found that individuals with strong social connections had a 50 percent higher likelihood of survival over the study periods compared to those with weaker social ties. This association remained consistent across various factors, including age, gender, initial health status, and cause of death. The study concluded that the influence of social relationships on mortality is comparable to well-established risk factors such as smoking and alcohol consumption, and it exceeds other risk factors like physical inactivity and obesity.

With such a strong connection to health, we can only conclude that humans are designed to be in relationships. Further, the high impact on health dictates that we find every opportunity to build relationships. Work relationships can be another source of connection and complement our personal relationships.

Research consistently shows a connection between relationships and health, so organizations are responsible for creating environments that foster these connections. A culture built on strong relationships is not just a moral imperative; it's a competitive advantage.

Obstacles

Unfortunately, many obstacles can hold us back from building strong, positive work relationships. A lack of a proactive approach to relationships magnifies these obstacles.[33] It is more difficult to address relationship issues than prevent them. When we let relationship issues fester, it creates negative emotions, feelings, and distrust. *Real*ationship-Driven Cultures is a proactive approach. Being proactive regarding relationships is not likely to completely eliminate relationship issues. However, it will reduce the frequency and severity of relationship issues. *Real*ationship-Driven

Cultures provide mindsets and approaches to resolve the problems in a healthier way.

Studies show that while strong work relationships significantly improve employee satisfaction, many organizations fail to invest in them proactively.[34] Workers often report that their relationships are overlooked until problems arise. According to research, 77 percent of employees consider workplace connections critical to engagement, yet many organizations do not take steps to strengthen these connections until challenges emerge.[35]

Research underscores the critical role of strong, trust-based relationships in enhancing workplace productivity, engagement, and overall well-being.[36] However, many organizations continue to prioritize traditional productivity metrics over relationship-building initiatives, leading to underinvestment in this vital area.

A Pew Research Center survey of 5,902 U.S. workers found that satisfaction with workplace relationships, both with managers and coworkers, is a significant predictor of overall job satisfaction.[37] This suggests that fostering healthy workplace relationships can lead to higher employee engagement and productivity.

McKinsey & Company highlights that relationships with management are the top factor in employees' job satisfaction, which in turn is the second most important determinant of employees' overall well-being.[38] This finding emphasizes the importance of cultivating strong relationships between employees and management to enhance job satisfaction and overall well-being.

Despite these insights, many organizations still view relationships as secondary to productivity metrics, resulting in underinvestment in relationship-building initiatives. By recognizing the profound impact of workplace relationships, leaders can implement strategies that foster trust and collaboration, ultimately leading to improved organizational performance and employee well-being.

Quantum Workplace research underscores how the emotional climate of the workplace is directly tied to the quality of relationships.[39] Poor relationships, marked by a lack of trust and respect, fuel negative emotions like stress, frustration, and disengagement. However, environments where trust thrives enable employees to feel valued and supported, reducing stress and fostering collaboration. Managers play a critical role in cultivating trust by addressing conflicts, promoting transparency, and creating a culture of open feedback.

These findings align with the idea that humans are biologically wired for connection. The ability to form and maintain trust-based relationships not only supports individual mental health but also drives organizational success. This underscores the argument that humans are inherently relational, and workplaces that nurture trust and relationships align with this fundamental design.

Ineffective communication is another major obstacle. Without open, honest communication, misunderstandings arise, which can erode trust and prevent collaboration. Some suggest that only about half of employees feel they have productive conversations with their managers.[40]

The shift towards remote and hybrid work models has introduced challenges in fostering strong interpersonal relationships among employees. Despite regular communication through digital platforms, the absence of face-to-face interactions can impede the development of meaningful connections, leading to feelings of isolation.

A 2024 survey by ResumeBuilder.com, which included 1,000 U.S. remote workers, found that 25 percent felt their social skills had declined since transitioning to remote work during the COVID-19 pandemic.[41] Challenges reported included initiating conversations, maintaining eye contact, and participating in group discussions. Additionally, nearly 20 percent of respondents reported worsened mental health, with social isolation being a significant contributing factor.

These findings underscore the importance of intentional strategies to foster connection among remote workers. Organizations can implement virtual team-building activities, encourage informal virtual gatherings, and promote open communication channels to mitigate feelings of isolation and strengthen workplace relationships.

In today's workplace, structured opportunities for connection are vital yet frequently overlooked. While many organizations implement systems like weekly one-on-one meetings, the data suggests these are often insufficient in fostering genuine relationships. A survey by Flowtrace found that 83 percent of employees spend up to one-third of their workweek in meetings.[42] Despite this, a significant number of employees report feeling disconnected from leadership and colleagues. This disconnect, as highlighted by the Society for Human Resource Management (SHRM), reveals that 66 percent of workers lack strong connections with their peers.[43] The issue is clear: organizations often prioritize productivity metrics over relationship-building, leaving employees feeling isolated and disengaged.

These findings underscore the need for organizations to go beyond simply scheduling meetings. To create a culture where relationships thrive, meetings must serve as intentional spaces for open dialogue, mentorship, and authentic connection. Regular one-on-ones, team-building activities, and transparent communication channels are not just add-ons—they are essential for fostering trust, collaboration, and engagement. By addressing these gaps, companies can unlock the benefits of stronger relationships, including improved morale, increased productivity, and reduced turnover. As workplaces continue to evolve, the importance of creating intentional connection cannot be overstated.

What to Do

There are great benefits to overcoming these obstacles and shifting to a more proactive, relationship-focused approach. Organizations can significantly enhance the well-being, engagement, and performance of their workforce. Since relationships undeniably impact our performance and health, it only stands to follow that they are important to organizational health.

Relationships have been an area of focus through organization development for some time now. Some examples include DiSC, 5 Behaviors of a Cohesive Team, Human Synergistics, and many other great tools. In my view, they will continue to be valuable tools to improve our organizational relationships.

However, I want to push us to go further and do more with how we think about and approach organizational relationships. We can proactively and systematically create environments where relationships get more guidance and increased prioritization. This is the best solution to get the inclusion we strive for. We can bring back the value of work and make our organizations places where employees want to come and can gain a sense of purpose and value from the work they do.

We are all driven by our deep-seated beliefs. What we truly believe about the world around us has a huge impact on our actions, behaviors, and decisions. I am suggesting Three Foundational Beliefs to guide us, but believing *our deepest purpose and greatest strength is relationships* is the most critical.

Relationships Are Core and Constant in Organizational Life

The Claim

Over time, organizations have changed in a few ways, including organizational structures, team structures, compensation, benefits, and in-office versus remote or hybrid work arrangements. The changes typically take place in search of efficiency, more employee engagement, and better results for customers. Differences and changes in these aspects are also based on the situation. What works in one industry or company may not be best in a different context.

Industries and companies can be different in many ways. Differences include company size, financial position, regulatory environment, product or service, and culture, to name a few. These differences inform the best structures and processes for a given situation.

In past years, organizations have become more hierarchical. The additional layers provided more oversight and control. This worked well for a while but also had a negative impact. Communications suffered as layers increased. It became more difficult to have a consistent message that reached everyone in the organization. Employee engagement also suffered as employees felt more micromanaged and less connected to the vision and mission of the company. In response, our organizations shifted to flatter hierarchies with fewer layers of management to increase engagement and employee ownership while reducing management costs.

Team structures have also changed. Organizations of the past did not even focus on "teams." They grouped employees into departments and thought of them as employees doing similar work. Around the 90s, organizations changed their view and focused on creating teams. In fact, that is what drew me into the work I do today. I worked at Harley-Davidson when the company shifted to a High-Performance Work Organization concept with self-directed teams. I loved the idea of shifting our view of organizational life.

Over time, team structures have morphed. We went from mostly intact, structured long-term teams to networked teams, project teams, and temporary teams. In today's workplace, you will likely be on multiple teams. I believe it's time for another shift. If we shift our focus from teams to relationships, we can create deeper connections between employees and build a stronger commitment to organizational goals. The improved employee experience will have a positive impact on company performance. As company hierarchies and team structures change and team members come on and off teams, employees' abilities to build and maintain relationships become even more critical to success. Relationships will always be part of organizational life, making them foundational to individual and collective success.

Support for the Claim

Organizational and Team Structures: Traditional departmental structures have increasingly given way to flexible, project-oriented, and networked team structures. For instance, many organizations now rely on temporary or project-based teams that form and dissolve as needed, which allows for agile responses to market changes but also requires adaptable relationships. This shift is evident in companies like Continuum, where employees cycle through networked teams, bringing fresh insights and fostering connections across the organization. However, constant restructuring of teams can challenge team cohesion, necessitating stronger interpersonal connections and collaboration skills to maintain performance and innovation.

Compensation Strategies: Compensation models have evolved significantly to adapt to competitive labor markets, inflation, and the shift toward remote work. A recent survey showed that 65 percent of organizations now use market-based compensation structures, up from 55 percent in 2019, with many adopting geographically adjusted pay for remote and hybrid roles.[44] Additionally, around 40 percent of companies have updated their compensation models to account for remote and hybrid arrangements, acknowledging that flexible work options are now integral to attracting and retaining talent. These changes reflect the need for new compensation strategies that align with the dynamic structures of modern organizations.

Work Locations (Remote and Hybrid): The workplace has undergone a shift in recent years, with remote and hybrid work models becoming central to how organizations operate. These changes reflect evolving employee expectations and the increasing importance of flexibility in the modern workforce. A 2024 report by Robert Half found that 37 percent of U.S. job seekers are interested in fully remote positions, while 60 percent prefer hybrid roles.[45] This data underscores a growing trend: employees value the ability to work flexibly, balancing the benefits of remote productivity with occasional in-person collaboration. Furthermore, the report highlights that 31 percent of professionals looking for new roles cite the desire for greater flexibility as a top motivator. These shifts have redefined not only where we work but also how we think about the concept of the workplace itself.

However, this shift has not been without challenges. While hybrid work provides flexibility, it often comes at the expense of spontaneous, in-person interactions that foster collaboration and innovation. A 2024 Forbes article noted that structured hybrid models have become the new norm, yet many companies struggle to maintain employee connectivity and engagement.[46] Reduced face-to-face interactions hinder relationship-building and, in some cases, create a sense of disconnection. To combat these challenges, organizations are making significant investments in digital tools like videoconferencing and project management software to replicate the collaborative environment of physical offices. These technologies aim to bridge the gap, enabling teams to stay connected and productive regardless of location.

These changes illustrate the transformation in how and where people work, but relationships continue to be foundational for productivity, innovation, and overall organizational success, especially as team dynamics and work environments become more complex. This data reinforces that relationships remain a core and constant element in organizational life, enabling teams to navigate evolving structures successfully.

Obstacles

Hybrid and remote work arrangements introduce unique challenges, intensifying the need for intentional relationship-building. For instance, remote employees often report feelings of disconnection due to fewer spontaneous interactions, like casual office conversations, which previously facilitated bonding and knowledge sharing.[47] This has prompted a need for deliberate strategies to build connections, such as regular check-ins, intentional social interactions, and transparent communication channels.[48]

In hybrid work environments, where employees might be both remote and on-site, fostering community becomes essential for collaboration and morale. Companies have found that scheduled informal interactions and inclusive practices, like virtual "co-working spaces" or social channels for remote teams, help mitigate feelings of isolation. Effective hybrid and remote collaboration require leadership to encourage open, inclusive communication and support structures that prioritize both professional and social connections.[49]

Previously provided research highlights that connection and trust within teams impact efficiency, engagement, and innovation. Without proactive relational structures, remote teams may struggle to reach optimal performance. Strategies such as intentional team-building activities and transparent project management have been shown to enhance remote team cohesiveness, underscoring that relationships are integral to organizational effectiveness regardless of structural changes.[50]

Changes in team structures from traditional departments to more flexible, networked, and temporary teams have significantly heightened the need for strong workplace relationships. Today, employees are often members of multiple, fluid teams—project-based, cross-functional, or temporary teams designed to tackle specific initiatives. This flexibility can improve agility and innovation, but it also presents challenges for building cohesive and lasting team relationships.

Temporary or project-based teams often form, disband, and re-form with different members, making it difficult for

THREE FOUNDATIONAL BELIEFS

employees to establish stable connections or a shared culture. A networked team structure, while offering flexibility, demands that employees quickly adapt to new team dynamics, communication styles, and collaborative technologies. This constant shifting requires more deliberate relationship-building efforts, as team members must often work closely with individuals from various functions or even other organizations, sometimes without ever meeting face-to-face.

What to Do

As organizational teams have evolved to prioritize agility and adaptability, the need for structured approaches to building and sustaining strong relationships has increased. These efforts are essential for unity and performance, allowing team members to navigate the complexities of multiple, shifting team roles while maintaining productivity and morale.

Through *Real*ationship-Driven Cultures, organizations can provide a structured, intentional approach that provides guidance and clear expectations and creates a shared understanding of strong, positive relationships. Building and maintaining good relationships become essential skills for employees. When individual performance is based on organizational success, self-serving behaviors are reduced, which creates the desire to build relationship skills and relationships.

Organizations Are a Collection of Four Key *Real*ationships

The Claim

Organizations are relationships. It takes collective effort to succeed in business. Strong, positive relationships create interactions that encourage cooperation, innovation, shared success, and meaning from work. Since these benefits are paramount to compete in business, it is easy to invest in strengthening our relationships. When we improve our relationships, we improve our organizations.

Viewing organizations as relationships assists our efforts to focus on relationships and make them a priority in our culture. This view goes beyond focusing on people. It connects employees to each other and the business at a deeper level, creating an environment where employees and the business thrive. Additionally, it goes further than a metaphor to think about organizations differently. Metaphors help us view things in new ways, see things from a new perspective, and increase our thinking flexibility. These can all be helpful. However, we want the Belief that Organizations Are a Collection of Four Key Organizational *Real*ationships to be permanent. When we use metaphors, it is typically to create new understandings. Used in the organization context, we can think of organizations "as" or "like" something else to push our understanding of how organizations work. Then, we go back to thinking of them as organizations. Our belief in organizations as relationships should be a deeply held belief that lives on.

Support for the Claim

Our third Belief is a natural extension of the first two Beliefs. The first Belief highlights the importance of relationships at a personal level. The second Belief focuses on the importance of relationships to organization success. If we buy into our deepest purpose being relationships and the importance of relationships in organizations, we will naturally view our organizations as a collection of relationships.

A quick examination of a typical work week easily reveals that organizations are a collection of relationships. As an employee, you likely have others on your team. You may provide them with work product. You may receive work product from them. Collaboration, problem solving, and decision making may also be part of your interactions. Similarly, you may have that same interaction with employees in other teams. This is the Employee-to-Employee relationship. No matter what level you are, you report to someone. Depending on your role, others may report to you. This relationship is the Leader-to-Employee relationship. If you are a leader, you will have peers from other departments or functions. You are likely on a team together. Hopefully, you are optimizing the greater good not suboptimizing your function. Regardless, you are in a Leader-to-Leader relationship. Finally, every company, by design or inadvertently, has systems, processes, approaches, and ways of working that impact employees' experience. This is the Company-to-Employee relationship.

Obstacles

This Belief is a natural place to discuss metrics. What gets measured, gets attention. If we believe organizations are a collection of relationships and they are important to both individual and organizational success, we will pay attention to them. Metrics are a way to create and keep focus on the key measures to impact results.

Sometimes organizations gravitate to financial, quality, and production metrics, taking the focus off people. Of course, these "hard" metrics are important and should be tracked and improved. However, it can't be at the expense of monitoring the health of relationships. Balance and focus should be on both. The health of relationships is more of a leading indicator for results. Whereas hard metrics tend to be focused on what happened in the past.

There are multiple factors that create an over-reliance on hard metrics. There tend to be forces that attract organizations to hard metrics and repel them away from soft metrics. To be clear, I am not trying to push us away from hard metrics. They are important to accountability and improvement. I am trying to create a balance. Many leaders believe that if financial, productivity, quality goals are met, everything else takes care of itself. I believe winning, or reaching these hard metrics, can repress people issues, but if they are there, they will come out during times of struggle. Alternatively, proactively focusing on employee relationships can increase your chances of reaching hard metric goals and overcome struggles in reaching them.

Leaders and therefore organizations gravitate towards hard metrics for several reasons. They are quantifiable, which makes them more verifiable. Hard metrics are easier to develop, measure, and track over time. Leaders tend to be more comfortable with hard metrics. In part, because of their financial, operations, and engineering backgrounds. Organizations are typically under pressure to deliver short-term results. Larger organizations, especially publicly traded companies, answer in part to stockholders and investors who are looking for short-term gains. Entrepreneurs rely on cash flow to cover both personal and business expenses, creating the need for short-term results.

We are repelled from soft metrics for several reasons. Improving relationships, engagement, and culture take time, so the results are not as close to when the work happens as compared to hard metrics. While research shows the correlation between strong relationships and business success, many leaders struggle to see the direct connection. We can measure our people improvement efforts, but it can be difficult to isolate the effects of the work. No matter how good our measurement practices are, soft metrics carry some level of doubt, making them seem less urgent. Hard metrics are seen as objective and reliable, while soft metrics rely on surveys, interviews, and observations.

What to Do

I will resist the temptation to go into great detail regarding metrics. I believe a balanced scorecard is the best approach. It should include both hard and soft metrics. One of my personal guiding principles is, everything exists in a context. This is especially true for metrics in organizations. It is important to follow good measurement practices, but your balanced scorecard will be unique to you. Additionally, you should consider measuring some specific interventions that are not part of the ongoing balanced scorecard.

It can be tempting to pick a few metrics quickly and start measuring. I recommend putting some thought into it and developing an overall strategy. When choosing metrics, we need to examine what behaviors the metric will drive. If we are not careful, we may unintentionally get behaviors we do not want. A well-known historical anecdote, often referred to as the "Cobra Effect," describes how British colonial officials in India implemented a bounty on cobras to reduce their population. However, this incentive led people to breed cobras for profit, ultimately worsening the problem. Economist Horst Siebert later used this story to illustrate unintended consequences in economic policy.[51] While the exact origins of this story are debated, it remains a powerful example of metrics driving counterproductive behaviors.

Other considerations should include how to gather measures. People measures typically come from surveys and interviews. They can include different primary purposes, including culture or engagement, large and small scale interventions, and talent management systems. You can measure things like training and development, engagement, trust, leadership effectiveness, employee experience, job satisfaction, to name a partial list. A caution is to not measure everything. Measurement takes time and effort, so an hour invested in measuring is an hour you are not doing something else. Choose wisely.

I have some general rules for measuring to make it effective and worthwhile. Only measure things that you will actually take action on. Don't measure everything you could measure. Only measure what you should measure. Sometimes, using two measures helps prevent the unintentional bad behaviors previously discussed. A simple manufacturing example is measuring the number of widgets produced as well as the first run quality of those widgets. This prevents producing without regard to quality.

A focus on relationships and people results should live in all your talent management processes and systems. I use the term Focused Talent Management. I am referring to making sure relationships are at the center of talent management. Performance Management should be a 50/50 split between what you did (results) and how you did it (relationships). In succession planning, only leaders who build and maintain great relationships should be considered for promotions. Development efforts should include relationship skills. Coaching, mentoring, and team interventions should include an aspect of creating good relationships.

CHAPTER 7

FOUR KEY ORGANIZATIONAL
REALATIONSHIPS

---

4 KEY *REALATIONSHIPS*

1. Employee-to-Employee *Realationship*
2. Leader-to-Employee *Realationship*
3. Leader-to-Leader *Realationship*
4. Company-to-Employee *Realationship*

Since relationships are our deepest purpose, have an inordinate impact on culture, and are a source of satisfaction, it only makes sense to view our organizations as a collection of relationships. Good continuous improvement dictates that we start with a clear understanding of what we want to improve. Therefore, we need to define what relationships we are working to improve. There are Four Key Organizational *Real*ationships that encompass the various types of relationships you can find in any organization: Employee-to-Employee, Leader-to-Employee, Leader-to-Leader, and Company-to-Employee.

Relationships are stronger when we have agreed to positive guidelines and mutually agreed upon purposes. Strong relationships are the lifeblood of organizations. Good relationships bring employees together to support each other and, in turn, the organization's success.

As an employee, you will have many relationships. Each of them will fall into one of these four categories. In order to improve and maintain our work relationships, we first define them so that we can understand them. Each of the Four Key Organizational *Real*ationships includes a unique dynamic and each has their own set of purposes.

Common *Real*ationship purposes give the individual relationships within an organization focus and something to strive for. Relationships with purpose go beyond having a common goal as being part of a team. Purpose has a deeper meaning and is more enduring than common goals. For instance, one of the purposes of the Employee-to-Employee *Real*ationship is "meaningful work." The idea is for employees to unite together to accomplish work that has a positive impact on company results. This purpose lives on even if the purpose of the team shifts, and it pushes purpose beyond narrow job descriptions.

Purpose brings people together and builds commitment to each other. It makes it easier to navigate differences within teams that may otherwise negatively affect relationships and, thus, the business. Purpose and connection make it easier to forgive small transgressions, easily resolve misunderstandings, and prioritize relationships.

Employee-to-Employee *Realationship*: Connect Employees

The Employee-to-Employee *Real*ationship has the most reach since everyone is an employee first. It doesn't matter what your level or function is or if you have a leadership role, you are an employee who interacts with other employees. This relationship sets the stage for positive interactions that are productive and satisfying.

The Employee-to-Employee relationship should connect employees to each other. The four purposes, represented by the acronym MODE, are designed to help employees focus on meaningful pursuits that strengthen relationships.

MODE

M	*Focus on Meaningful Work*
O	*Prioritize Organizational Success*
D	*Desire to Change*
E	*Embrace Realationships*

Meaningful Work

Good work relationships focus on meaningful work. When we are focused on accomplishing something of value, it brings us together. It builds excitement and creates a positive mindset. As we accomplish the work together, we create value in our relationships. When our relationships have value, they are more likely to be positive and continue. As we collectively accomplish meaningful work, the organization is more successful, creating more positivity.

Running into barriers as we accomplish work can actually be unifying. How we respond to adversity is an opportunity to build stronger relationships. If we deal with setbacks and obstacles in a positive way, resist the temptation to blame each other, and work to prioritize the relationship, our connections will grow stronger.

When we focus our interactions on meaningful work and come together to advance the organization's objectives, self-serving politics is reduced. Organizational politics has been shown to disrupt meaningful work, which serves as a mediating factor between politics and other negative outcomes such as burnout and reduced employee engagement. When employees perceive their work as less meaningful due to political interference, their motivation and involvement decrease, damaging team cohesion and interpersonal relationships.

These findings suggest that reducing self-serving political behaviors in organizations can significantly improve relational dynamics, reduce stress, and increase engagement, fostering a healthier and more productive workplace environment.[52] [53]

Meaningful work is simply the work of the organization. Leaders should communicate and employees should understand the value of the work they do. It can sometimes get lost or forgotten. Employees can underestimate the importance of their work. No matter what the contribution is, it has meaning. Explicitly and specifically recognizing everyone's worth creates focus for the Employee-to-Employee *Real*ationship. Seek to understand the value of every job and every employee.

Organization Success

One of the most damaging things in organizations is self-serving behaviors. We have all seen the leader or High Potential who prioritizes their success over others. The *Real*ationship-Driven Cultures approach has several methods of reducing self-serving behaviors, which is included in the Employee-to-Employee *Real*ationship because caring about each other's success in our relationships with other employees is the best remedy to combat the unhealthy focus on self.

Self-serving individuals are easy to recognize but hard to overcome. They spend an inordinate amount of time managing up—time that could be spent collaborating on better results. To boost their career, they blame others for mistakes and take credit for successes. Self-servers focus on getting things done. However, their attention is generally narrowly focused on things that will advance their career as opposed to organizational benefit and the success of others.

I am not suggesting that employees should not focus on their own success and career. I am suggesting that they are better served, especially in the long run, by focusing on the success of the organization and others. Focusing on serving the macro levels is a good way to ensure balance. Consider your impact and the value you add in a hierarchical way. You should think in terms of company, function, department, team, and self. The idea is not to completely ignore your own success, just to gain your success through Service to the greater good. As you add value to others who, in turn, add value and ensure your actions support the organization's success, you become more impactful and valuable. Maximizing value and impact on the organization is the best way to build your career.

Desire to Change

The Desire to Change purpose is two-pronged. It includes the desire to adjust behavior to improve our relationships with others. It also consists of the desire to participate in and advance organizational change. Change is part of our personal and organizational lives. Some people embrace change more easily than others, but we all have heightened awareness during change. We tend to ask ourselves, "Is this change good or bad for me?" "Can I be successful after the change is implemented?" "What is my role after the change?"

I love the quote by John C. Maxwell, "Change is inevitable. Growth is optional." It is a great reminder that change will happen with or without us. It is better to embrace change and try to influence it if necessary. The second part of this quote is a great reminder that change is a great opportunity to learn. Depending on the change, we may be able to learn new skills, gain new knowledge, or learn to adapt to changing environments.

When I work with individuals and teams to improve or repair relationships, I often use tools to help them understand human behavior. No matter what tool I use, I get commitment from them to apply the learning. As I stated earlier, knowing is good; doing pays the bills. In this situation, I recommend a three-step process as a path to take action and make the relationship better.

1. Understand yourself.
2. Understand others.
3. Adjust how you interact.

Turning the understanding into action is what this *Real*ationship purpose is about. It doesn't mean we change who we are. It does mean we adjust to what others need. If both employees in the relationship do this, synergy happens.

Having a Desire to Change is extremely important in today's organizations. Factors like technology, competitors, and the marketplace are only a few examples of things that are changing at quicker rates as compared to previous years. Change has become constant. Most of the time, organizations have multiple changes happening simultaneously. When employees generally embrace change, especially if they rally around change together, change does not seem overwhelming. Employees get a sense of being in it together. Problems and barriers are easier to overcome with a positive mindset, and more people are working through any issues that may come with change.

Embrace *Real*ationships

Embracing *Real*ationships sets the tone for how you interact with others. If you prioritize relationships, you are likely to do things that maintain them. If relationships are not important, you will ignore key things that help build relationships.

Disagreements will always be part of our relationships both at work and in our personal lives. When we embrace relationships, we disagree differently. We tend not to make the disagreement personal and do our best to avoid personal attacks. The focus is on the content of the disagreement, which makes it more likely that the conflict will be resolved productively. Disagreeing in this way is likely to improve the relationship.

Research by psychologist John Gottman has demonstrated that how couples handle disagreements can predict marital success or divorce with notable accuracy. In a study involving 95 newlywed couples, Gottman and his team conducted oral history interviews to assess each couple's relationship dynamics. They found that how partners discussed their relationship history and managed conflicts could predict, with 87 percent accuracy, which couples would remain married and which would divorce within four to six years.[54]

Gottman identified four negative communication behaviors, termed the "Four Horsemen of the Apocalypse," that are particularly detrimental to relationships:

1. **Criticism**: Attacking a partner's character rather than addressing specific behaviors.
2. **Contempt**: Expressing disdain or superiority over a partner.
3. **Defensiveness**: Rejecting responsibility and deflecting blame.
4. **Stonewalling**: Withdrawing from interaction and refusing to engage.

The presence of these behaviors, especially contempt, was strongly associated with marital dissatisfaction and an increased likelihood of divorce.[55]

Further studies by Gottman revealed that couples who maintained a ratio of at least five positive interactions for every negative one were more likely to have stable and satisfying marriages.[56] This "magic ratio" underscores the importance of positive communication and conflict resolution in sustaining healthy relationships. These findings have significantly influenced marriage counseling practices, emphasizing the need to address and modify destructive communication patterns to enhance marital stability.

Although work relationships are not as intimate as marital relationships, these concepts are still very applicable. They provide guidance that protects the relationship even in times of extreme disagreement. The four negative behaviors to avoid, identified by Gottman, provide details to the general advice of "attack issues, not people." The negative behaviors tend to be escalating, making the interaction more damaging. Because the behaviors are very personal, they generally elicit a negative response from the other person. As things escalate, it soon becomes impossible to resolve the original issue.

Small things remain small. When we value our relationship with someone, we are not irritated by small frustrations. There are billions of people on the planet, yet no two are the same. This suggests that we can be different in many ways. Therefore, it can be easy to be frustrated with others as they do not behave the same as we do. Of course, we start with the assumption that our way of behaving is the correct way. The more we cherish our relationship with someone, the more willing we are to assume good intentions. This assumption drastically improves our interactions with others. We increase the quantity and quality of conversations when we assume good intentions.

I coached an executive who struggled with assuming good intentions. Instead, he overwhelmingly assumed bad intentions. He became a client because he struggled to have positive relationships with others in his organization. We were searching for the underlying reasons for his struggle when we discovered one significant mindset that was getting in his way.

He worked in a company that relied on projects to accomplish their work. He has a Dominant personality type that is focused on results and taking action quickly. Many of the employees who worked for him were Conscientious personality types, which are analytical and reserved. Their approach to working was much different. He had a strong desire to complete tasks, make decisions, and move things forward. They strongly desired to ensure accuracy, gather data, and be precise. Instead of seeing the value of accuracy, data, and precision, he assumed they were slow, lazy, and unproductive.

Since it can be difficult to have a conversation about laziness, he avoided having the conversation. Had he assumed good intentions, it would have been an easier conversation. Eventually, he learned about different working styles and could more easily assume good intentions. More conversations brought better relationships. Better relationships allowed for both perspectives to be considered, contributing to better outcomes. He was able to advocate for action and decisions. Others were able to advocate for taking time to gather data and ensure accuracy.

Overcoming Barriers

People don't always think of work relationships as relationships. Organizations tend to focus on teamwork. Promoting good teamwork is healthy. But treating our work relationships as *Real*ationships goes deeper. In my observation, employees usually think of being in a work relationship with those they like, which is really a friendship. And for those they do not like, they just think of them as annoying coworkers to avoid. Friendship is not required to have strong working relationships. It is a bonus when those we work with become friends.

We should treat all our work relationships as *Real*ationships. Like our non-working relationships, we will have different levels of connection and enjoyment from different coworkers. If we are going to make maximum contributions to the organization's success, we must work to build strong relationships with all fellow employees. Using these four purposes as the focus for our work *Real*ationships, we can build connections and be productive even with those we do not want to build a friendship with.

Leader-to-Employee *Real*ationship: Leaders' Commitment to Employee Success

I am sure you have heard the old phrase, "People leave their boss, not the company." The day-to-day interaction and unique qualities of a given leader create an increased impact on the Leader-to-Employee *Real*ationship. A leader is responsible for the success of the employee. I tell every leader I work with that they cannot earn their paycheck through their individual contributions. Of course, every leader at every level has contributions that they must individually make. However, those are table stakes. To truly contribute as a leader, you must impact and optimize your team's contributions. By building strong Leader-to-Employee *Real*ationships, you can synergize the contributions of the entire team.

The Leader-to-Employee *Real*ationship is guided by the leader's commitment to creating an environment for his/her employees. The leader's commitment includes four key elements, represented by the acronym DECS, that provide the purposes for the Leader-to-Employee *Real*ationship.

DECS

D	_D_evelopment
E	_E_mpowerment
C	_C_ollaboration
S	_S_hared Risk

Development

Development remains a high priority for employees. A Gallup study indicates that nearly nine in ten millennials consider professional development or career growth opportunities to be very important in a job. Furthermore, "career growth opportunities" is cited as the number one reason individuals change jobs.[57] Employees want to work at companies willing to invest in their development. Development comes in many forms. It can be a formal training class, short video, project, or assignment. The leader's job is to start with good development conversations with each of their employees and match company needs with employees' desires.

Good development is a great retention tool as well as a way to improve company performance. As employees develop, their capabilities grow, allowing them to increase their performance and contribution. When the performance of individual employees increases, company performance increases.

Career development should be part of the development equation. This may be a high or low priority, depending on circumstances and individuals. Every leader should know the career aspirations of their employees. It starts with a career dialogue to determine what the employee wants and what is possible.

I recommend having a formal process to improve the quality of the discussion. For employees focused on career growth, the career dialogue should continue throughout the year. Career discussions and follow-up can be part of the performance management process or a separate process. The important thing is to be consistent and provide feedback on progress.

Coaching should also be part of the Leader-to-Employee *Real*ationship as a way to develop employees. Coaching should be a regular part of the interactions between managers and employees and should go beyond just career development. The coaching tool is particularly beneficial during Empowerment and Shared Risk, but can help in any learning situation.

Empowerment

Empowerment provides multiple benefits for both employees and organizations and often leads to development. Giving employees assignments that stretch their skills creates learning opportunities and builds experiences that can be applied to new situations. Over time, this practice builds employees' confidence in their ability to handle complex tasks and solve problems independently. Employees build decision-making skills as they are trusted to navigate and complete work with less oversight. These enhanced skills and decision-making capabilities benefit both the individual and the organization, as a more skilled and confident workforce contributes to higher performance levels and better outcomes. Empowerment is also a strategy enabler, though it is not always seen as such. When leaders take on tasks or decisions that could be delegated, they reduce their capacity to focus on the long-term success of their organization. Effective empowerment allows leaders to free up their time for strategic thinking, planning, and innovation. It also ensures that decision-making is distributed throughout the organization, allowing more agility and responsiveness in dynamic business environments. When I consult with organizations on building a more strategic approach, empowerment is often a key factor. Leaders who successfully empower their teams are better able to focus on crafting strategy, driving innovation, and steering the organization toward long-term goals.

Another benefit of empowerment is its positive impact on employee engagement and job satisfaction. Research shows that employees who feel empowered are more engaged, productive, and committed to their work. A Gallup study found that only 30 percent of U.S. employees feel engaged at work, but this figure increases significantly in organizations where employees are empowered to take ownership of their roles and decisions (Gallup, 2020).[58] Empowerment strengthens the Leader-to-Employee *Real*ationship, creating an environment where employees feel valued and respected.

Collaboration

Collaboration is a great way to bring more ideas to projects, problem-solving, and decision-making. It is an opportunity to bring diverse ideas together and ensure more complete solutions. Leaders should encourage and create opportunities to collaborate within and outside their teams. As leaders bring groups together to collaborate, it is important to empower them to the greatest extent possible. No matter what level of empowerment is given, it should be clear to everyone and adhered to.

Collaboration is an important tool in creating a *Real*ationship-Driven Culture. It shows up in three places. First, here in the Leader-to-Employee *Real*ationship. Second, it shows up in the Company-to-Employee *Real*ationship in Chapter 7. Third, it will be shown in Chapter 8, the Environmental Element of Involvement. Although the overall goal and purpose of collaboration remain consistent, there are differences in how collaboration is impacted based on the *Real*ationship and Environmental Element.

The leader's role in collaboration is to promote, encourage, and support it. Any good change agent knows the change stops in the leadership hierarchy wherever the change is not supported. If the CEO through the director-level support collaboration, it will happen at those levels. If the manager level does not support collaboration, it will not occur or at least not happen well. This means we need to make collaboration part of leadership expectations at all levels.

I will cover the role of the Company-to-Employee *Real*ationship and the Environmental Element aspects in more detail later in this chapter and in Chapter 8, respectively. For now, the company's role is to provide resources and processes to support collaboration. The Environmental Element of Involvement creates thinking patterns, approaches, and cultural expectations.

Shared Risk

Taking risks is important for innovation and employee development. However, it can be uncomfortable and scary. It can be difficult to get employees to take risks. Fear of a poor performance review, reduced responsibilities, career impediment, or even firing can prevent employees from taking risks.

Empowering employees to take calculated risks is essential for fostering innovation and creativity within organizations. When leaders create an environment that encourages risk-taking, employees feel more confident to explore new ideas and challenge existing processes, leading to innovative solutions. A Forbes article emphasizes that leaders who embrace creativity, encourage risk-taking, and foster a supportive environment are likely to drive significant change within their organizations.[59]

Sometimes, companies do not even realize their impact on reducing risk. While working with a senior leadership team for a large manufacturing company, I was asked how they could increase risk taking. I asked them, "How have you encouraged risk taking, and what happens when someone fails?" They shared many examples of how they communicated and encouraged risk taking. But stated, "Bryan, they don't take risks no matter what we say."

I reminded them of the second part of my question, "What happens when someone fails?" They seemed to give it serious consideration. Then responded, "Nothing." I pushed further. "Are you sure?" After further consideration, "Yeah, nothing." I answered, "Well, we can introduce some tools to assess risk and share information regarding risk-taking mindsets. Let me give it some more thought and come back to you."

Since risk taking was not on the agenda, I moved the group to the next topic. We navigated a few more topics and a brave VP interrupted, "Remember that time John's project failed, and he was moved to a small location and given an insignificant assignment?" Everyone nodded in agreement and a few other leaders remembered other examples.

I thanked them for their honesty and told them that it would be our biggest hurdle to overcome. To address this, I developed the concept of shared risk. It was the leaders' role to be involved in the risk. They were required to accept equal responsibility with the employee. It created a partnership to assess the risk and create an equal commitment to making it pay off. We provided training and tools to assess and manage risk, identified the points in the process where risk was more acceptable and where it had more severe consequences, and even created a "Best Failure" award. But sharing the risk gave us the biggest gains for increasing risk taking.

Overcoming Barriers

Sometimes leaders over-rely on personal connections with their directs. Over the years, leaders have been encouraged to make personal connections with their direct reports. The recommendations included getting to know their children, spouses, and outside interests as a few examples. Of course, this is a great idea. The caution here is that leaders should not make the Leader-to-Employee *Real*ationship overly reliant on personal connection. The relationship needs to maintain a level of professionalism with a focus on business results. Additionally, employees need to receive benefits from their work beyond a paycheck.

* * *

When leaders focus on these four purposes, their actions provide opportunities for employees to learn and grow. This leader's commitment to employees' success is the foundation for employees to give and receive value. The employee builds knowledge, skills, and abilities that will serve them well as they advance in their career. The company derives benefit from the deliverables as employees take ownership, collaborate, and take risks. As employees develop, the company wins by having more skilled employees.

Leader-to-Leader *Real*ationship: Leaders Work Toward Organization Success

How well leaders work with each other is critical to organizational success. When there is synergy and cooperation among leaders, the business wins. Decision quality increases, continuous improvement thrives, and change is adopted when leaders work well together for the benefit of the overall business.

The Leader-to-Leader *Real*ationship sets the tone and example for culture and how well employees work with each other. In my experience, employee behavior mirrors leadership behavior. If leaders are uncooperative and work in silos, so do employees. Employees overwhelmingly watch what leaders do more than listen to what they say. So, strong, positive Leader-to-Leader *Real*ationship not only impacts the leadership team but also has a direct impact on employee behavior. The four purposes are represented by the acronym TEAM.

TEAM

T	*Team Synergy*
E	*Encourage Improvement*
A	*Align on Change*
M	*Model Greater Good*

Team Synergy

When we look at team development, there are two basic aspects to consider. Task behaviors include getting results. Interaction behaviors include how well the team works together. Left on their own, teams typically focus only on task behaviors and ignore interaction behaviors. Team synergy plays a key role in results. How the team interacts impacts decision making, job satisfaction, engagement, results, and long-term success. Teams that take the time to assess and improve how they work together outperform those who ignore team dynamics.

The approach to focusing on team interaction behavior can vary. There are many different assessments available to fit various situations and needs. Some are more complex and some are simple. Using assessments is a good idea when you need anonymous feedback, need to uncover unknown issues, or members lack the skill to address issues on their own. Assessments can introduce new ways of thinking, approaches, and models, which can help improve team performance.

Informal check-ins, team performance discussions, and ongoing feedback are good ideas. They can provide benefits in between more formal sessions or might be enough for high performing teams with good team interaction behaviors. The key is to intentionally spend time on improving team interaction behaviors. Discussions about the team's ability to work well together can be sensitive, which makes us want to avoid them. However, if you make it part of your routine, it becomes less scary and easier.

How a leadership team interacts has two significant impacts. First, it directly impacts the performance of the leadership team. To get the best results, team members need to work well together, be able to challenge each other, and prioritize overall business success. If they can't, it is unlikely that they will make the best decisions, find the best solutions, or focus their efforts on the most important issues and challenges.

Secondly, I have found that leadership teams' interactions and approaches trickle down. How the leadership team goes, so goes the organization. The same or similar behaviors show up through multiple channels. Since the leader operates that way, the same behavior will likely be accepted and even encouraged. If silo-protecting is the norm for the leader, it will be mimicked by direct reports. If the focus is on collective results, that trickles down too.

People tend to believe what they see more than what they hear. If the leader promotes and coaches more positive behaviors than they are modeling in their team, employees are more likely to follow the behaviors being modeled than the behaviors being coached.

Encourage Improvement

A continuous improvement mindset has multiple aspects to it. It can be applied to the organization in general through many tools and approaches. It can also be used formally for specific processes and areas of the business. The aspect I will explore here relates to a leader's mindset with their peers. Although formal Continuous Improvement tools and methods may end up being applied, it all starts with a mindset that desires to be better, even if it means being vulnerable and admitting shortcomings.

Opportunities to improve are often initially raised as complaints, which makes us feel like we are being judged or even attacked. Complaints can be frustrating because they are usually judgments and generalized, which makes them less actionable. A productive way to deal with a complaint is to ask questions to understand the underlying concerns. With this level of understanding, searching for solutions and improvement can start. It takes patience, a greater good mindset, and strong *Real*ationships to have deep, challenging conversations to continuously improve.

Within a leadership team lies the opportunity to combine functional expertise, outsider view, and internal customer perspective. As the team explores ways to improve, they can share opinions outside the function to reduce blind spots. The internal customer view can identify opportunities to improve deliverables and service through a deeper understanding of needs and expectations.

It is important to remember that the leadership team should focus on collectively making things better for everyone. The leader's primary objective should not be to solely advocate for his/her function, which can lead to sub-optimization and blind spots.

Align on Change

Today's organizations are in a constant state of change. Leaders who have the skills and mindset to navigate change well add a lot of value. Managing change is a team sport. It is important for leaders at all levels to work together on change. They need to create consistency in messaging and overall support of the change. When I lead change, I encourage the leadership team to create a list of non-negotiables. This list is an agreement and will receive unwavering support. Changing the decisions should be extremely rare and only if you learn something new and extremely damaging, if the decision is not revised. The list should be high-level and due diligence should be done to ensure that it is the correct path. Then, everyone fully commits even if all their ideas were not accepted.

For example, a company may decide to implement project management software. After using data to determine the ROI of the investment, gathering data from key stakeholders regarding pros and cons, and completing an RFP to select the best option, a final decision is made to purchase project management software. Typical decisions that would end up on the non-negotiable list include the fact that you are implementing the software, the software that was chosen, who is and is not required to use the software, who can use the software if they want to. This representative example list gives you an idea about the things that the leadership team would be fully committed to. When resistance comes up, it is worked through, but the items on the list are not up for discussion.

Leaders need to honor their commitment to each other, the organization, and the success of the change. When employees complain about the change, it is tempting for leaders to open every decision for discussion. However, that is not a good use of time and energy. It may also set up the false expectation that those decisions are open to debate. Then, when the decision is not reversed, the employee feels like the leader did not listen to them. A better use of time and energy is to set the non-negotiable decision aside and point out the areas where empowerment does exist.

When an employee brings complaints about the new software and wants to kill the project or just not use the software, you should set that aside early in the exchange. Simply state, "The decision to implement this software has been made. I am sorry you are frustrated. Let's talk about your concerns and find a path forward." Shifting the focus to what can be changed most of the time creates a positive interaction and identifies areas of empowerment and actions that can improve the implementation.

Most, if not all, change has areas where employees are empowered and where they are not. It is important for the leadership team to identify, commit, and communicate these areas. Left on their own, employees tend to focus on areas where they did not have empowerment. From the previous example, if they do not like the software, they will focus on the fact that they were not involved in the decision to implement project management software, and which software was chosen. They may lose sight of their areas of empowerment, which typically include additional training, how to transfer current projects, and how their department may divide the implementation actions.

When leaders commit to each other and lead change effectively, change adoption increases. The speed, quality, and benefit realization also improve. Additionally, leaders with good change skills like influence, communication, and relationship building do better to lead change. With change being a larger part of organizational life, how you manage change has become increasingly important and has a huge impact on employee experience. Employees do not distinguish between leading and leading during change. They simply experience leadership. Since change is frequent, how you lead during change is critical.

Model Greater Good

As previously discussed, self-serving behaviors are very disruptive to organizations. It is crucial for leaders and leadership teams to prioritize modeling the greater good over self-serving behaviors. The focus needs to show up in decision-making, communications, and talent management, including being a key factor when promoting employees to higher levels.

Although implementation isn't always linear, a good prioritization list includes company, function, team, and individual. Each situation is worthy of analysis and thought, a good practice is to prioritize the highest level impacted. Using this approach creates the most value and drives more strategic decisions. In the end, individual needs and wants are addressed by serving the greater good. It can be difficult for some to see that connection and have the patience to allow individual success to come to fruition.

Overcoming Barriers

One of the more common struggles is how leaders approach being on a team with their peers. Do they come to the table only to promote and represent their function? Or do they have the mindset that they are there to run the overall business, and their function is a piece of it? The latter mindset is needed to optimize overall business results and break down silos.

In most cases, the leader who overly focuses on their own function does so with good intentions. The leader wants to optimize their area of responsibility. Making each function operate well is generally good. However, no matter how successful a company is, resources are limited. Therefore, at times, choices must be made when allocating resources. Considering the impact on the overall organization ensures long-term success.

Being overly competitive can also get in the way of leadership team synergy and focus on overall organizational benefit. We all like to win. If we focus on self-serving wins, it can impede wins for the organization. Friendly competition among peers can be fun and motivating. However, we have to remember that the success of the overall organization is everyone's responsibility and the most important priority. Reminders, discussions, and organizational-level scorecards keep leaders focused on the greater good. If additional intervention is needed, executive and team coaching can help leaders understand the importance and build their competence in making their function and the organization successful.

Company-to-Employee *Realationship*: Systems/Processes to Engage Employees in Running the Business

The Company-to-Employee *Realationship* is built on the premise that all employees should be involved in running the business. There are many roles within a company that contribute to its success. When all employees are fully engaged, the company is more successful.

Although well-intentioned, I dislike the statement, "Employees are our biggest asset." In a way, it places employees in the same category as machines, buildings, and other balance sheet assets. Even if the company structure is not such that all employees have formal legal ownership, all employees collectively are the company. Having a systematic way to bring employees together to bring the strategy to life is what the Company-to-Employee *Real*ationship is all about. The four purposes make up the acronym CALL.

CALL

C	*Collaborate*
A	*Align*
L	*Lead*
L	*Learn*

Collaborate

Company-to-Employee *Real*ationship collaboration consists of systems and processes to improve collaboration. It's essential to implement systems and processes that foster open communication, clarity, and efficiency. Consider the following systems and processes to improve collaboration.

- **Communication Platform:** Some examples include Microsoft Teams or Zoom. By having a centralized platform, you increase the visibility of all things related to the project or work. It eliminates scattered emails and the need to monitor multiple channels, which creates more transparency and alignment. It also increases the speed of communication through chats and direct messaging. The ability to get quick answers and decisions ensures the work continues seamlessly. Providing updates in a single platform ensures progress is shared and remaining action items are clear.

- **Project Management:** Some common, easy-to-use systems include Trello, Asana, and Monday. There are more complex software options for those that have higher requirements. Project management is essential in planning the work. If you have a good system, you can start with a more complete plan. As the work progresses, it is easier to determine where you are in the project and make adjustments along the way.

- **Document Sharing:** Some great tools include Google Workspace, Microsoft 365, Confluence, and Notion. These tools allow work to be done simultaneously, eliminating the need to work in sequence with other team members. Document-sharing tools build a real sense of co-creation. They also help with version control and the need to email documents back and forth.

- **Knowledge Management:** Some tools here include SharePoint, Confluence, or Notion. Depending on the type of collaboration or project, you may need to share knowledge, best practices, or updates. When you have the need to share information or knowledge outside of the team or longer term, knowledge management systems can help. They make it easy to store and organize large amounts of knowledge and make it accessible and searchable to a large number of employees.

- **Meeting Management:** Using agendas, having clear meeting roles, timeboxing, and follow-up action items all help ensure you make the best use of your time in meetings. Employees complain about meetings mostly because they are not viewed as work or necessary to get the job done. You can change that by making sure meetings are actually focused on getting work done. Be sure to only include employees who will be part of decisions, information sharing, or can provide special knowledge.

- **Clear Decision-Making:** Decision processes are also beneficial to great collaboration. It is important to define the types of decisions and who will make decisions up front. This clarity makes sure everyone is on the same page and prevents conflict later. I have seen employees get really upset when they are told, or it is implied that they will be the decision makers, only to find out that it was only true if the leader agreed fully with their decision.

- **Governance:** Having a well-defined governance process is also best practice. Most projects that benefit from collaboration are complex and involve multiple functions within the company. Sometimes, there are external consultants that create additional complexity. Determining who is the overall lead, who will lead different workstreams, and who has the final decision for a given decision area should all be part of the governance plan. If any decisions are the responsibility of a team or committee, you should define who breaks the tie or overcomes any sticking points.

- **Accountability:** A great, well-known tool to create clarity and accountability is RACI, which defines roles and responsibilities. Agreeing and documenting roles and responsibilities helps avoid duplication of work, increase ownership, and build commitment. If we know who is responsible for what, it makes it easier to hold employees accountable and keep the work on track.

Align

Getting employees to row in the same direction and cadence is necessary for organizations to thrive. It is not enough to develop a great strategy. You must implement it, communicate it, and keep it top of mind as work happens. The only way to bring the strategy to life is through employees. The first step is to communicate the strategy. If employees are going to align with it, the strategy must be communicated through multiple channels and be available for reference.

A good communication strategy includes cascading a consistent message through all levels of the organization. Each level must evaluate how their work impacts the strategy. Goals, daily work, and decisions should be considered and aligned with the higher-level strategy. Frequent check-ins to review progress, remove barriers, plan for upcoming work, and adjust as needed, keep the strategy active and increase chances of success.

Too many companies spend time developing a strategy but do not communicate it effectively or follow through.

It can be a lot of work, especially in today's business environment, where change is constant. Strategies do not last as long as they did in the past. They need to be adjusted more frequently. The answer can't be to shortchange our strategic processes. We must get more agile with strategy development, deployment, and follow-up. Strategy is as important as it has ever been, so getting better at it helps us lead organizations successfully.

Systems and processes like the company intranet, performance management, including goals, one-on-one ins, and project plans, should all be leveraged to implement and track progress to strategy. Having strategy built into systems and processes already in place makes it easy to monitor progress, make adjustments, and evaluate performance to accomplish the strategy, goals, and objectives.

Lead

Leadership plays a critical role in all organizations. In most organizations and situations, teams behave very much like their leaders. Most leaders I have worked with drastically underestimated the amount of impact they have. They typically assume that the team's behaviors are separate from their own. One of the more extreme examples of this happened at a major corporation I worked with. I was brought in to help transform the organization. Three functions had been combined into one, but they very much still operated as three separate functions. The leader was frustrated and brought me in to bring them together.

The goal was to convince employees that they should act as a single function. I was not there long when I realized I would have to convince the leadership team to act collectively first. They were operating in silos and were overly protective of their respective functions. Little consideration was given to the overall synergy and collective results.

I was fortunate to be working with a senior executive who was open to hearing that the senior leadership team was the problem. We used assessments, 360 feedback, one-on-one interviews, and team and individual coaching to bring the senior leadership team together. The process made them realize that they were not behaving in the way that they were asking the organization to operate. After some intense work and reflection, they started operating as a team, and the organization followed.

Setting clear leadership expectations ensures consistency. Employees desire consistency in leadership. Consistency in leadership reduces surprises and increases fairness. When employees know what to expect from leaders, they are more prepared to meet those expectations. Although leaders should have their own style and personality, organizations should have guidelines and priorities regarding how leaders lead. When you create what good leadership looks like for your organization, you create consistency, which increases fairness.

Learn

Organizational survival requires learning. Things are constantly changing and evolving. Your competition is always trying to get better. To keep up, organizations must invest in learning. Type, size, industry, product, and services are some of the factors that play a role in creating a learning strategy and supporting systems and processes. Each organization is unique, so learning needs vary. The right strategy ranges from sophisticated, formal systems and processes to very informal systems and processes. Any situation can benefit from spending time developing a learning strategy based on a formal needs assessment.

The biggest mistake I see is not having a learning strategy. It is important to understand what you need to be successful, develop a strategy, and invest in the right solutions. Without a strategy, you are likely to either not invest in learning or invest in the wrong things. Even if you do not have the resources to fully invest in all identified needs, a strategy helps you prioritize. It is better to be strategic about what you invest in based on a solid strategy.

No matter what your learning strategy reveals, all organizations can benefit from two learning tools: coaching and feedback. These learning methods help drive continuous, daily learning. They are inexpensive and do not require a lot of time.

In many organizations, feedback is an underused tool. Feedback is typically very quick and timely and can be impactful. It allows learning in the moment or at least close to the moment. It creates a lot of learning with little investment. The reasons some people hesitate to provide feedback include concerns about rejection, fear of defensive or aggressive responses, and confidence in their own abilities. To overcome this, we can share more effective methods of giving and receiving feedback. We can also make feedback part of the culture. Feedback should be an expectation as we carry out our work.

Coaching is another great daily, continuous learning tool that can be fairly inexpensive. In this case, I am not referring to formal coaching with a professional coach and a contract. There are many types of coaching, but here I am talking about the manager as a coach. At times, a highly trained coach with a formal contract is a great tool. However, for situations that require more than feedback but less than formal coaching, having leaders skilled in coaching can be a great answer.

When direct reports need more than feedback, being able to coach them is a great option. It can be helpful to turn performance around, try out new behaviors, or learn a new skill. In most cases, leaders and managers do not naturally have coaching skills. They can greatly benefit from some training. They do not need to become fully certified coaches with hundreds of hours of training. A simpler approach can yield great benefits. Providing basic coaching skills can give leaders what they need to impact the performance of their direct reports.

I built my career during the time when coaching became a prominent tool in organizations in the '90s. I was and still am a big believer in coaching. I am glad to have played a small role in advancing the practice of coaching. As head of talent management, I always implemented a formal coaching practice. It is beyond the scope of this book, but all organizations should have a coaching strategy. Coaching strategy should include an organizational approach and a manager approach.

Helping People Change is a great book to explore options and strategies.[60] The book does a deep dive on coaching approaches and benefits. The book provides research-based insights that will provide guidance on coaching strategies for your context. Additionally, it explores the impact on relationships. An important finding related to our topic of relationships includes, "These relationships often sustain themselves over long periods of time because the people develop deep, resonant relationships involving mutual caring and compassion, shared vision and purpose, and an upbeat, helpful mood.

Overcoming Barriers

The biggest barrier to the Company-to-Employee *Real*ationship is having a coordinated strategy that is sustained over time. In many companies, talent systems and processes are implemented separately over time. In my experience, companies do not take the time to infuse a well-coordinated strategy based on a consistent talent philosophy. Companies tend to look at best practices for each tool and process. Another barrier is that employees lose sight of why systems and processes are in place over time. Managing talent becomes an HR activity employees are "required" to complete.

*Real*ationship-Driven Cultures provide a coordinated, consistent philosophy for talent management. The dual focus on results and people is foundational to having success as a company. The Company-to-Employee *Real*ationship ensures that systems and processes are tools for running the business more effectively, not HR processes. To ensure that those systems and processes do not lose their luster over time, the Talent Management group must onboard new employees systematically and remind everyone periodically why we have them. Sharing success stories and monitoring the quality of usage will also help make the time invested in talent activities valuable.

CHAPTER 8

FOUR ENVIRONMENTAL ELEMENTS

```
┌─────────────────────────────────────────────┐
│  ╭─────────────────────────────────────╮     │
│  ( 4 ENVIRONMENTAL ELEMENTS ──────────●       │
│  ╰─                                           │
│      1. Mindsets                              │
│      2. Purpose                               │
│      3. Involvement                           │
│      4. Service                               │
│                                               │
└─────────────────────────────────────────────┘
```

A key factor in moving from relationships to *Real*ationships is the environment. Conformity theory shows us that people will change their behavior to fit in with the group. Using this concept, we can create an environment that influences decisions and choices that eventually create a culture focused on *Real*ationships.

In the Milgram studies, a test subject worked with a fake researcher and a fake test subject.[61] [62] The task was for the fake test subject to learn a list of words and be able to repeat them to the test subject. If the answer was incorrect, the test subject was to push a button that shocked the fake test subject. The fake researcher and the actual test subject were in one room, while the fake test subject was in another room.

The shock was not real, but the fake test subject made it sound real by screaming. The fake shock was supposedly increased with each wrong answer. The fake test subject screamed increasingly loud with each incorrect answer. The shock levels were clearly identified, yet many test subjects went to dangerous and even deadly shock levels. They were told they would be paid even if they quit the exercise, but should continue in the interest of the overall experiment, the data, and learning from it.

It was concluded that people were willing to shock their fellow test subjects, in part due to the perceived authority of the researcher and in part because they wanted to be part of the overall research experiment. The Milgram studies showed that we can impact behaviors and outcomes through conformity theory. We use the influence of authority and the desire to be part of the group to create positive behaviors and outcomes. By creating an environment of strong, healthy relationships, we impact organizational culture to be unifying, create self-worth, and, therefore, be resilient.

Another famous study comes from Solomon Asch.[63] His study was simple yet enlightening. He had a researcher lead a group of fake test subjects and one actual test subject. The task was to identify the longest of three lines. The fake test subjects gave their answers first, and the actual test subjects always came last. The fake test subjects conspired ahead of time as to which wrong answer they would provide.

Overall, 74 percent of the actual test subjects gave at least one wrong answer to go along with the group over twelve trials. Twelve percent of the participants gave the wrong answer in almost all tests. If we can get people to go against their nature to be correct, we should certainly be able to get employees to go along with creating a culture of strong, healthy relationships.

These two studies highlight that people want to be part of a group and are willing to change their behavior. It is why we concentrate on and overwhelm the environment to make *Real*ationships a way of life. With strong, healthy relationships as our foundation, we are free to pursue the success of the company. We can disagree productively, challenge each other to be accountable, free our creativity to be innovative, and have relationships we enjoy. Our relationships and work are focused on company success, not relationship navigation and stress.

Mindsets: How We Treat Each Other

Central to nurturing organizational *Real*ationships is the adoption of specific Mindsets. These Mindsets act as guiding principles, illuminating the path towards more meaningful and effective interactions. Imagine an organization where every individual approaches their colleagues with empathy, openness, and a collaborative spirit. Such mindsets do not merely enhance interactions; they transform them, fostering a climate of mutual respect and understanding. The Mindsets are represented by the acronym CARLS.

CARLS

C	Commonality Transcends Differences
A	Actions Enhance Words
R	Realationships Matter Most
L	Long Term Nice
S	Service Over Self-serving

Commonality Transcends Differences

When we think about what makes us human, we often focus on what sets us apart. Our differences, while real, are not easily influenced. They include things like where we were born, our race, our height, or the culture we grew up in. They shape our individual stories and have meaning but don't define what connects us. If we take the time to analyze our human experience, we see a truth that's often overlooked: What we share as humans is far more profound and impactful than what separates us.

The list of what we have in common is probably longer than you think. It's filled with elements that touch the deepest parts of our humanity. Although it may play out differently, we all love our families. We all strive to seek connection, have a desire to be valued, and want to be understood. We crave safety, fairness, and a sense of belonging. Having an impact and living a meaningful life may have different definitions for each of us, but we all do our best to accomplish them. These things are universal, transcending the boundaries that often divide us.

What's even more powerful is that most of the things we have in common are within our control. Listening to others is a choice. We can create safety and foster trust. Acting with fairness, showing empathy, and helping others feel valued are things we can all do to build connection through commonality. These are choices we make every day, no matter who we are or where we come from.

Compare commonalities to our differences. Some of our differences include things like our height, the country we were born in, and the color of our skin. They are static and beyond our influence. We didn't choose them, and we can't change them. While they shouldn't be ignored, they don't have to dominate how we see ourselves or others.

When we focus on what we have in common, we shift our perspective. Instead of barriers, we see bridges. Instead of division, we find connection. Our shared humanity is deeper, richer, and more unifying than any difference we may have.

Our shared traits and desires are the foundation for building stronger, more meaningful relationships. They remind us that we are more alike than different and that focusing on commonalities is one of the most powerful ways to create connection and understanding. By choosing to see and act on what connects us, we open the door to deeper relationships.

Deep connections make it possible to disagree on important, sensitive topics and maintain a strong relationship. Rallying around our common human elements helps us prioritize the relationship over our differences and disagreements. At work, being able to disagree openly and productively increases creativity and innovation.

I am not suggesting we ignore our differences. In fact, I like a common phrase that has been popular for a while, "celebrate our differences." I think that is good advice. Differences add flavor and fullness to our relationships. In organizational life, differences can be catalysts for creativity, innovation, and effective problem-solving. Our deep connections on a human level allow us to fully explore and leverage our differences.

I realized this while completing my master's degree at Case Western Reserve University. Part of that program was to study in universities and consult with companies across Europe. Before we left for the trip, we were given an assignment. After our trip, we were to write an essay on the cultural differences of the various students and employees that we would meet. The European students had the same assignment.

During our free time, many conversations started by exploring cultural differences. Those conversations were fun, interesting, and enjoyable. However, after we exhausted the list of differences, the conversations naturally drifted to what we had in common. None of us purposely set out to discuss what we had in common. It just naturally happened without us truly realizing it.

I noticed the energy shift during those conversations. People were more excited. They smiled more. They listened more. They shared more. There was a distinct difference. After noticing this, I started discussing our commonality earlier in the conversations. The energy was always higher, and people were always more eager to talk about their children, family, contributions at work, and volunteer activities. You may have noticed the list contains things that connect us with others, which bring us back to relationships.

Overcoming Barriers

Focusing on commonality can be difficult, especially in organizational life. What started as "celebrate our differences" has become "focus on our differences." A reminder that differences are good is healthy. An obsession with differences can divide, segregate, and create friction. Too much of a good thing can be bad.

In my lifetime, I have seen society and business shift from a heavy focus on differences to less focus on differences and back to a heavy focus on differences. In 2024, we saw a return to overly emphasizing differences. Some colleges implemented segregated dorms and graduations. A city official held a Christmas party for nonwhites only. She was so confident in her decision that she disinvited whites after accidentally inviting them. These trends are troubling and counterproductive.

We must resist the tendency of social media, media, and some organizations to focus on differences to the point of division. Coming together through commonality is a better approach. After all, we are all human. I designed *Real*ationship-Driven Cultures to create Unity and Self-worth. The Commonality Transcends Differences Mindset paves the way for building Unity in our work relationships.

There is a business benefit of bringing employees together. "Social capital—the networks, relationships, shared norms, and trust among individuals—is the glue that holds organizations together. When teams feel connected, they tend to get more work done and do it faster. When colleagues trust their managers and one another, they tend to be more engaged, more willing to go beyond minimum work requirements, more likely to stick around, and, as research shows, more likely to recommend that others join their organization."[64]

The benefits are universal, further showing it to be a humanistic norm as opposed to a cultural norm. A Gallup study shows that regardless of culture or geographical location, strong relationships are consistently linked to improved life satisfaction and workplace performance.[65] This research confirms the benefits for both our personal and professional lives.

Actions Enhance Words

Most of us are familiar with the phrase, "Actions speak louder than words." They encourage us to take action. Another common saying, "Talk is cheap," reminds us that without follow-through, words alone can lack substance. Both expressions point to the importance of acting, not just speaking.

While the advice is sound, it's incomplete. Our Mindset, Actions Enhance Words, takes the advice a step further to create synergy between action and words. The most meaningful impact comes when words and actions are aligned.

Words have undeniable power. They can tear down or lift up. Of course, we encourage using them to inspire, uplift, and guide. Words can offer encouragement, share wisdom, or provide direction. But words alone, though impactful, often fall short when action is needed. For example, if a team member is struggling, offering words of encouragement is helpful, but stepping in to roll up your sleeves and help them overcome obstacles speaks volumes. Going beyond verbal support, actions amplify the impact of words.

There are times when words alone are sufficient, such as when they allow someone to work through challenges on their own to foster growth. In these cases, well-chosen words can encourage without interfering, providing just enough support to inspire confidence. However, we must make sure it is in their best interest that we choose this strategy. The decision to not support with action should not be based on our lack of commitment or self-centeredness.

Another aspect of this Mindset deals with consistency between actions and words. For example, if you are a leader who says they empower employees but don't assign meaningful tasks and decision authority, your actions are not enhancing your words. Employees will soon understand that you do not truly empower them. If you tell your employees to respect each other but you do not show respect to others, your words become empty.

Employees are watching what you do, not listening to what you say. When not congruent, actions will always be believed over words. Furthermore, you are better off to say what you will do even if it isn't popular. If you do not intend to empower employees, just say it. You will be respected more for saying what you will do and doing it even if it is not popular. For instance, it is better to say, "I will not empower you," and live to that than to say, "I will empower you," and not do it.

Overcoming Barriers

Sometimes, we hesitate to support others with actions because of our workload. Of course, we have to make sure we keep our commitments and complete our work on time. However, that rationale sometimes becomes an excuse. To overcome this barrier, think in terms of the "right amount" of supportive action to provide. You do not need to take over the task. Provide enough action to move them forward.

None of us are perfect, and many of life's situations are complex, so our words and actions won't always line up. However, it should be a rare incident, not a consistent occurrence. Self-exploration and reflection help you understand your core beliefs that drive behavior. We all naturally tend to act in alignment with our deeply rooted beliefs. Therefore, when learning new concepts or approaches, I recommend exploring how they fit your current belief systems. You also need to understand and explore how the new information fits your context.

For example, maybe you read about empowerment and decided to be an empowering leader. It sounds good and could positively impact your team, organization, and leadership capabilities. You will want to explore what barriers prevented you from empowering your employees in the past. Two common barriers I see when I coach executives are the fear that it will take longer with reduced quality and the underlying belief that the employee cannot learn to do the work effectively and efficiently. With those beliefs, you cannot see the long-term benefits of empowerment. To empower others effectively, you will need to shift your beliefs that your employees want to and are capable of learning.

The thought process in this representative example can be used to align words and actions in any situation where you are struggling. Understanding what belief is driving your behavior is the first step to deep behavior change.

Re*ala*tionships Matter Most

In our interactions with others, it is critical that we prioritize the relationship. This philosophy isn't merely a nice-to-have; it's a strategic imperative that can redefine the dynamics of interaction, collaboration, and conflict resolution. If we value relationships more than anything else, it changes how we interact with others. Our disagreements tend to not turn personal. We are more likely to attack the issue, not the person. When we disagree in this way, we can debate issues passionately yet maintain the relationship.

Prioritizing the relationship also helps us to avoid the relationship-destroying mistake of picking a position in a debate and defending it no matter what. Position-picking reduces or eliminates listening and causes us to pile on arguments that may not be logical or true since our only goal is to win the argument. If we value the relationship above winning the argument, we become more curious, which leads to increased listening. It may even cause us to ask questions and explore the validity of the other side(s) of a disagreement.

It can be difficult to keep the relationship as the highest priority in the heat of the moment. Sometimes, we get passionate about a topic or a solution we have proposed, kicking in our competitive spirit. It can be easy to have that competitive spirit morph into a win-at-all-cost mentality. Work relationships can be especially difficult. At work, credit for an idea or solution can have an impact on career opportunities. That impact can include higher visibility projects, pay increases, or even promotions. Employees with a short-term and or self-serving approach are particularly vulnerable to losing focus on prioritizing the relationship. They can easily be sidetracked by the lure of a quick raise instead of longer-term, more sustainable success.

Something I love to do is build on ideas I disagree with. The next time you are in a meeting and someone suggests an idea you disagree with, provide three things you like about the idea. I have been known to say, "I don't think I agree with your idea, but let's talk about the pros or benefits of implementing it." It shows that you are willing to listen and explore ideas. If, in the end, you and the group still disagree with the idea, the person feels heard and you have more fully explored ideas.

The approach provides several benefits. People feel more part of the group and more connected to others when they feel heard. The group builds the habit of exploring ideas for pros and cons instead of dismissing them without discussion. Exploring ideas is an essential element of innovation. And, you may just find yourself perfecting an idea you disagree with to the point it is the best option. Rarely is there a perfect idea, so building a pros and cons list is a great habit to build.

*Real*ationships Matter Most is foundational, and the Mindset that will build connections that are difficult to break. When we genuinely care about others, we want them to succeed, which builds lasting Unity. Being concerned about the success of others does not prevent you from reaching your personal career goals; it enhances your ability to impact the organization positively, increasing your chances of advancing your career.

Overcoming Barriers

It is easy to forget about the importance of relationships, especially at work. We get preoccupied with building our own careers, finishing a project, or having our ideas win. Although strong, positive relationships are likely to benefit our career and work, we sometimes do not remember that in the moment. By remembering that our deepest purpose is relationships, we improve our interactions with others. We cheer on everyone's success, debate issues passionately and respectfully, and are enriched by our relationships.

There are some common mistakes that pull us out of the *Real*ationships Matter Most Mindset. These errors typically creep in as the conversation progresses. We set out with the intention of maintaining the relationship, but as things progress, our goal for and our approach to the interaction shifts. If no one recognizes and addresses that the interaction is off track, things escalate.

- **Pick a position and defend:** We overcommit to our original idea and lose our curiosity. Winning becomes the goal.

- **Assuming the intention of others:** We assume others have negative intentions and we have only altruistic intentions.

- **Opinion bias:** We hear someone's opinion on one topic, put them in a group, and assume all their opinions fit that group.

- **Perfect solution error:** Assume either your solution or some solution comes with no downside. Most times this is false. It is extremely difficult to find a perfect solution.

- **Different definition:** Working from a different definition regarding the same topic. This typically happens with complex topics or topics that have different definitions for different people.

- **Create an opinion:** We define others' opinion for them, versus trying to understand their opinion, and then argue against it. We typically define it in an extreme form, making it easier to argue against.

These common mistakes can be solved with a few strategies. One of the most helpful things is to remain curious, truly seek to understand. Many times, it is emotions that get in the way. If you can recognize when emotions are escalating both for yourself and others, you can step out of the conversation and address how you are having the conversation. Make the goal to learn not to win. And finally, always remember *Real*ationships Matter Most. Ask yourself throughout the interaction, "Am I advancing the relationship or harming it?"

Long-Term Nice

Long-term nice is a critical yet hard-to-accomplish Mindset. This Mindset could also be called Challenge with Love. I first used the phrasing long-term nice early in my talent career. I thought of it after reflecting on a coaching engagement. It reinforced the importance of being direct and honest even when it is difficult.

I had just started coaching a VP of HR at a Fortune 200 company when he shared a situation that had been troubling him. Just prior to our coaching engagement, he terminated one of his employees. He regretted having to let him go even though the employee's performance made it necessary. He was fond of the employee, but the employee was struggling to interact positively with others in the organization. His behavior was causing issues, so the VP put the employee on a performance improvement plan. The plan did not work, and the employee was terminated. The HR leader shared that he was extremely confident that performance would turn around with the plan and was surprised it did not work.

I started with questions to explore the most likely problems, assuming the performance plan and coaching should have worked.

- Did you set clear expectations?
- Did you provide direct and accurate feedback?
- Did you set a regular meeting schedule for you and the employee?
- Did you both keep all the meetings?
- Did you hold yourself and the employee accountable?

The VP responded yes to all the initial questions. I suspected he believed his answers were accurate. I also suspected that his memory needed some jogging, and his definition of clarity, direct feedback, and accountability may be different than mine.

I asked permission to challenge him. The VP truly wanted to learn and agreed to extensive, detailed questioning. As I questioned him, I realized my suspicions were accurate. It took him longer to come to the same realization. Eventually, he said, "Oh, I wasn't very clear. I was not very direct, and I did not hold him accountable." I could see the disappointment in his face and hear it in his voice. He knew he missed an opportunity to help the employee.

I tried to comfort him by sharing that the way he dealt with the performance plan was common. It's why most performance plans do not work. Handled properly, performance plans can be a great tool to motivate, inspire, and coach improved performance. All Four Environmental Elements and all Five Mindsets in *Real*ationship-Driven Cultures are helpful in Performance Improvement Plans. However, Long Term Nice is the most critical and the most difficult to accomplish.

Since the employee was already let go, the only thing left to do was learn from the situation. I asked why he was not clear regarding expectations, not direct with feedback, nor assertive with holding the employee accountable. He started listing reasons, "I didn't want to demotivate or demoralize him. I didn't want him to fail." I pushed him further, "What did you want most?" He replied, "I wanted to be nice!" In a kind, playful voice, I asked, "Well, how nice is it now? He is fired." The VP agreed that although he was being nice at the moment on a short-term basis, the long-term effect was the opposite of nice.

I use this example often when I am trying to convince leaders to make the uncomfortable choice of being direct, challenging, and focused on accountability. Many times, a leader's attempt to be nice causes issues for the company and the individual. There is a false belief that you must choose to be direct or nice. That is a false choice. There are two separate choices to make. If you think of the choices as being on two continuums. On one continuum is Direct vs. Indirect. On the other is Nice vs. Mean. Of course, there are variations between the extremes. As you can predict, I am going to suggest choosing spots close to the ends of Direct and Nice.

A modern barrier to Long-Term Nice comes from technology. With the invention of the internet and the advancement of phones came what I call the echo chamber. People now have the ability to get unchecked support for almost anything. There are many different types of groups for almost anything you can imagine. Many of these forums create a victim mindset where challenging each other is forbidden.

Echo chambers cause two major problems. First, at the macro level, some of the online groups promote behaviors that in the past would have only remained fringe. With immediate and unchallenged access to harmful behaviors, mindsets, and viewpoints, poor choices are amplified instead of being left to fade away or be challenged. This has led to harmful mindsets becoming more normal, creating a negative impact on society.

Second, at the micro level, the individual can escape the need to think critically and challenge themselves. Going to the echo chamber only reinforces the individual's mindsets, behavior, and decisions, no matter how bad they are. Prior to echo chambers, the individual would have likely come in contact with multiple people who would challenge them. When people challenge each other, they tend to refine their thinking and adjust their behavior, making healthier decisions.

In extreme cases, people can isolate themselves from real interactions and spend an inordinate amount of time in the echo chamber, reintroducing poor choices and behaviors. The bottom-line result is a culture that views challenging each other as a negative. As this mindset becomes more prevalent, we find it showing up in our organizations.

Organizations that do not have the ability to challenge each other, processes, and policies will not survive. They will be overtaken by organizations that do challenge each other. Continuous improvement is essential to survival and mandatory to thrive. A quote by the late Joe Paterno comes to mind, "Today, you've got a decision to make. You're gonna get better, or you're gonna get worse, but you're not gonna stay the same. Which will it be?" This quote highlights the fact that your competition is working hard to get better, making it impossible to maintain the status quo. If you are not improving, your competitor's improvement is making you worse off than you were yesterday.

If you truly value challenging each other, you will see the challenges as an act of caring for the individual and the company. Respectful challenges are the catalyst to improve both individual and company performance. Strong relationships make it easier to challenge each other. Building relationships over time makes it easier to challenge a coworker. You are more at ease and willing to share your intentions for improvement as opposed to ridicule. They are more willing to hear the challenge because they assume your intentions are good. This reduces defensiveness and increases acceptance in hearing the challenge.

Overcoming Barriers

Conflict avoidance prevents us from giving needed constructive feedback. Our fear of offending others prevents us from helping them. If you have a strong relationship with the person prior to providing sensitive feedback, it typically goes much better. How you deliver feedback also increases the chances of success. If they trust you and believe that you have their best interest at heart, they will listen, not be offended, and at least consider what you have to say.

If we lack confidence in our interpersonal skills, we may hesitate to provide direct feedback. Our fear of not being able to navigate the defensiveness that may come from giving feedback that is critical, can force us into silence or overly sugarcoating the feedback. That is why good interpersonal skills are so important. When we are comfortable navigating our own emotions and the emotions of others, we confidently focus on being Long Term Nice.

Sometimes having a strong relationship puts us at risk of not prioritizing the relationship. We may take the relationship for granted or get complacent. I suggest finding ways to remind yourself of the relationships you have and the value they provide. Make them part of your gratitude journey. You can share with others that you are grateful for the relationship.

Service Over Self-Serving

While working with organizations across the globe, I have found that one of the most detrimental behaviors is self-serving individuals and teams. The Mindset of Service over self-serving brings the concept of service directly to the relationship. The concept of Service is found in various aspects of a *Real*ationship-Driven Culture. In the context of a *Real*ationship Mindset, it is a reminder that we are at our best when we prioritize the success of others and the organization.

Service unites us because it is an act of caring. When we start with service to another person, team, or organization, it shows that we are focused on the greater good, which builds trust and brings people together. At the team and organization level, a Mindset of Service improves our ability to solve big problems and overcome obstacles. With more people focused on the team and organization, there is more energy and brain power to achieve great things.

Our own success is an outcome of focusing on the success of others. The best way to be valuable is to add value to others and the organization. If our time and effort are focused only on our own contributions, we impact the contributions of one person. If we focus time and effort on the success of others, we compound our efforts and increase our contribution to organizational success. Our individual success is enhanced through serving the greater good.

I will cover the organizational role in Service later in Chapter 8. When the organizational environment supports serving the greater good, it enhances service at the personal level. However, the responsibility still lies with employees living out a Mindset of Service.

Having the right beliefs and attitudes is critical to making service a natural way of working. Three important personal approaches include humility, empathy, and gratitude. Humility is foundational to believing others have ideas and opinions worth hearing and considering. Empathy creates connection through understanding and care. Mutual care creates an environment where we want to help each other. Gratitude creates a sense of satisfaction, which reduces pressure to advance at the expense of others. We can strive for more while being grateful for where we are.

Overcoming Barriers

Many things get in the way of having a Mindset (and heart) of Service. Some are external, and others are internal. I will start with external. We are constantly told to focus on ourselves. As a way of being customer-centric, many companies create processes, products, and services that are tailored to the individual consumer. In a company-consumer relationship, this can be positive. Probably the most famous example is Burger King. A tagline they use often is "Have it your way." When it comes to ordering a burger, getting what you want is a good thing. In fact, this is an example of BK serving customers. However, in our organizational relationships, this mindset can be detrimental to the greater good of the organization. If we are consistently trying to "have it our way," we are putting our needs and desires ahead of the team, function, and company's success. Selfishness damages trust and, therefore, relationships.

Additionally, our ego and pride can prevent us from having a heart of service. Many of the behaviors that manifest as pridefulness and egotism can be useful behaviors that benefit us and others. The problem arises when we exhibit behaviors in the wrong amount, in the wrong situations, or with the wrong perspective. Below are some internal barriers to a service mindset.

- **Competitiveness** can be a powerful motivator, but it needs to be channeled and directed in the right way, especially in organizational life. It should not be, "I need to win." It should be "We need to win" when it comes to working in organizations. A great example that illustrates this thinking comes from an exercise I ran in organizations for many years. The exercise came from MIT. It is an interactive, competitive game.

  The basic premise is that participants are put into several separate teams. The rules are simple.

  - "Win all you can."
  - Only talk to your team.

  There are ten rounds where the teams make decisions that result in winning/losing money by choosing an X or a Y. There are a few rounds where you let the teams talk to each other. The payout scheme for the decision results is structured so that everyone wins a small amount if all teams choose X. If only one team chooses X or Y, and everyone else chooses the opposite, the highest dollar amount is rewarded. There are different combinations of winnings based on the different choice possibilities. The teams have the payout scheme, so they could easily reach the conclusion that for everyone in the room to win, teams all have to choose X.

I ran that exercise hundreds of times. Every time, teams interpret the goal to be that their team, not all teams, are to "win all you can." There were a few times when teams came to that realization during the rounds when the teams were allowed to talk with each other. Unfortunately, without exception, there was always at least one team that double-crossed the agreement for all teams to vote X.

As you may have guessed, the debrief compares the teams to organizational functions like operations, finance, human resources, etc. The teams collectively represent the company. The group then explores real-life silos and opportunities to work more synergistically together. It is easy to get caught up in winning all you can in organizational life. We over-emphasize our function, looking to optimize our piece of the business. We can get caught up in our own career aspirations. If we don't take a step back, consider the big picture, and remember the ultimate goal is to excite our customers, we can sub-optimize the overall company.

I am not suggesting that the participants are bad people. I participated in the exercise prior to facilitating it. I acted in the same way. It is a natural approach. The exercise highlights how easily we can frame our competitiveness in an unproductive way. That is where strong relationships come in. If we care about the people we work with and value our relationships, we are more likely to celebrate their wins and find ways to support them even if they work in a different function.

- **Self-centeredness** is likely the closest to being the complete opposite of the Mindset of serving others. A self-centered person believes everyone exists to provide for their needs. This approach damages trust. When you interact with a self-centered person, it is obvious that they will do anything to advance their own agenda. They do not hesitate to use you to get what they want without regard or concern for you. The self-centered employee is not likely to focus on what is best for the company or customer. The focus is on self-image and self-benefit.

  *Real*ationships stress greater good, which demands that we make decisions that serve the big picture. The individual is rewarded and gains value and benefits from serving the customer, company, and function above self. Additionally, *Real*ationships require you to place a high value on building and maintaining relationships. By valuing relationships, you automatically remove extreme focus on self.

- **Defensiveness** is the killer of feedback, which is a critical continuous learning tool. Employees and leaders with defensive tendencies don't take feedback or accept difficult truths. They have the attitude that "I am in charge" and or "I am always right." Other employees learn not to challenge them and are likely to reduce or stop providing feedback. Defensive cultures are not learning cultures. They lack the ability to challenge ideas and debate solutions. Generally, decision quality goes down.

When our goal is to serve others, it is easier to reduce defensiveness since we are thinking of the greater good and not our own ego.

- **Entitlement** can also impede a Mindset of Service. An employee who feels entitled thinks, "They owe me. I earned it. I have been here long enough." The entitlement mindset leads to self-centered behaviors. The focus moves away from the greater good and making sure everyone wins. It becomes all about personal needs. Having an entitled attitude most likely comes with or leads to a self-righteous attitude, where the employee thinks they are better and, therefore, more important than others. Of course, this returns the focus to self above others.

- **Critical spirit** is someone who is always looking for what is wrong. Nothing is ever good enough. Identifying problems can be helpful in improving our organizations. There is a difference between pushing to make things better and being critical about everything. A critical spirit opposes everything, even if the idea or solution has merit. Further, this person doesn't typically provide alternative or better ideas. They just squash everyone else's ideas.

- **Extreme Independence** describes an employee who wants to do everything on their own. They avoid teamwork and collaboration. Some employees just prefer to work alone, and some think their individual accomplishments will lead to success. Problem-solving, creativity, and innovation all suffer when too much independence exists in organizations.

We can all fall victim to these behaviors since they all serve a positive purpose. For example, defensiveness is part of our self-protection mechanisms. So, being defensive helps us survive and protects us from both physical and mental threats. However, if we are overly defensive when receiving feedback, we miss an opportunity to learn. The Service Mindset puts us in the right frame of mind to enrich self-worth in ourselves and others. Understanding the internal barriers listed above provides the knowledge we need to shift to Service.

Purpose: Why We Work Together

Purpose Is Multi-level

For me, purpose has multiple levels. Some are deeper than others and, therefore, have more meaning. When we recognize and understand the different facets of our purpose, our lives have more meaning, flavor, and nuance. Life Purpose receives the most attention. It is talked about in general conversations and social circles. Some people make a living helping others explore and determine their life's purpose. It is certainly good to connect with life's purpose, but we should go beyond that to holistically understand our purposes. Purpose is an Environmental Element as part of *Real*ationship-Driven Cultures. We will explore all aspects of Purpose, which include deepest purpose, life purpose, vocational purpose, and organizational relationship purpose.

Deepest Purpose

At the heart of our discussion regarding purpose lies a profound truth: The deepest purpose of humans is to be in a relationship. This is not merely a philosophical stance; it is a principle that resonates deeply within the human experience. In the organizational context, our work relationships can contribute to our deepest purpose. They may be different than other relationships, but we should not underestimate their value.

Work relationships will not be as intimate as our spousal and familial relationships. Although work relationships can turn into friendships, they typically won't be as close as our personal friendships. The goal isn't to turn our work relationships into personal relationships. If it happens, it is a bonus. We should strive for good working relationships and make an effort to strengthen them with all our coworkers. We can find deep meaning in our work relationships and create connections through joint problem-solving, striving for common goals, and collaboration. If we follow good relationship management practices, the source of satisfaction, accomplishment, and connection is even stronger.

I have worked with teams that struggle with the concept that work relationships do not have to be friendships. Some people do not see the value of investing the time and effort to build relationships with coworkers with whom they would not be friends. This thought process is damaging in several ways.

First, you miss an opportunity to have more relationships. Second, the team does not function as well as it could. Teams thrive when members invest in each other and prioritize everyone's success. Finally, overall company performance may suffer from poorer-performing teams. Since our purpose is also tied to our role and company, we miss an opportunity to add more purpose and meaning to our lives. Being in relationships is our deepest purpose and is constant throughout our lives.

Life Purpose

The most common definition or focus on purpose comes from our calling in life. Sometimes, our life purpose is conflated with our vocational purpose. Although they can be somewhat connected, I view life purpose and vocational purpose as being separate and only a portion of our purpose. If life purpose and vocational purpose are inextricably linked and our only purpose, we have a problem if we are no longer able to work in our vocation.

For example, healing may be your life purpose, and you may work as a nurse in a hospital. In this case, your vocation and life purpose are linked and aligned. If something unfortunate happens to you and you can no longer work as a nurse, it does not mean you no longer have a purpose. In multi-layered purposes, you still have your deepest purpose. You can still maintain your relationships. You may be able to teach other nurses. You would be fulfilling your life purpose of healing while working in the vocation of teaching. In this case, your life purpose and vocational purpose are somewhat linked. You are teaching others who will then fulfill their life purpose of healing.

Depending on circumstances, you may no longer be able to even loosely connect your life purpose to your vocational purpose. In this case, you might fulfill your life purpose through friends and family and fulfill your vocational purpose through some other means. However, even if you can no longer work, you still have a purpose. You have your deepest purpose of being in a relationship, and you may be able to fulfill your life purpose of healing through non-work avenues.

I think vocational purpose can change over our lifetimes. Sometimes, we have a life calling or purpose that is lived out through different avenues. If you are a healer, you may live that out by directly treating patients. Then, you might move into a hospital leadership role. Your focus is still helping people heal, but your role in that changed. To effectively run a hospital and heal people, both roles are needed.

Others may change vocations completely. Over time, we can seek out new challenges or have our passions shift. Some career shifts are subtle, and some are drastic. The key is to determine the "whys" underneath "what" you are doing. Why do you like it? Why do customers benefit from what you are doing? Why does the company exist? These why questions help you understand the value behind the work.

Vocational Purpose

Vocational purpose includes your job, function, and company, and can also provide meaning in your life. When these are in sync with your life calling, the synergy can be a great source of fulfillment. If they are not in sync, your job may not hold as much meaning, but it is still a great source of purpose and meaning.

All companies serve some purpose. The fact that the company has customers shows that someone values what the company provides. Your company may provide essentials of life or just something fun. It may be a product. It could be a service. No matter what it is, the customer perceives value.

Circumstances permitting, there is a great benefit to connecting life purpose with vocational purpose. Research shows a strong correlation between passion for one's work and higher job satisfaction, as well as reduced stress and burnout.[66] When individuals are passionate about their jobs, they tend to experience lower levels of emotional exhaustion and are better equipped to cope with job-related stress.

One study found that harmonious passion—where individuals engage in work they love and feel intrinsically motivated by—serves as a protective factor against burnout.[67] Employees who score high in harmonious passion have greater intrinsic job satisfaction, even under high-stress conditions, such as physical fatigue and emotional weariness. This suggests that being passionate about one's work can mitigate the negative effects of burnout and maintain job satisfaction despite challenging work environments.

Additionally, research highlights that finding meaning in one's work not only increases job satisfaction but also boosts motivation, engagement, and overall personal fulfillment.[68] This, in turn, leads to reduced absenteeism and lower stress levels.

Promoting a work culture that fosters passion and aligns with employees' personal values can, therefore, lead to better job satisfaction and lower stress levels, even in demanding job roles. For some people, and in some situations, the connection to purpose is more obvious than for others. Companies can help employees connect with purpose by articulating the value they provide and sharing the impact they are having on customers and the world. It does not have to be something that is done daily, but should be done periodically.

It is important to understand what your specific tasks are, but you should look further to understand the impact of your work.. Know what the overall result is and how it impacts the customer. What is the final product or service that you are a part of creating? Understand how the product or service will be used, what value it provides, and why people purchase it. This is not a play on words or tricking yourself into a false belief. Even tasks that seem simple and not consequential have meaning.

For example, someone who makes burgers at a fast-food restaurant may underestimate their value. They may view the task as repetitive with limited value. However, thinking deeper about the role will reveal its value. The person making the burger adds an important piece to the overall sandwich. The sandwich may be part of a larger meal, which could include fries and a drink added by others who contribute to the meal. The person who purchases the meal receives value by getting a quick meal. Maybe it is the difference between eating and not eating. The customer may have extremely limited time that day. Because the team each completed their role, the customer was able to have a meal and complete all their tasks.

Realationship Purpose

Additional purpose comes from leveling up your work relationships to *Real*ationships. Each of the Four Key Organizational *Real*ationships has its own set of purposes. The specific purposes and their meaning are covered in detail in Chapter 7. Giving each of the Four Organizational *Real*ationships purposes provides additional meaning to those relationships. *Real*ationship purposes create Unity by giving direction, meaning, and focus. When we understand why our relationships are important and how to focus our energy, we are less frustrated by differences and less irritated by our human idiosyncrasies. We build rapport and connection, making our work relationships enjoyable and a source of satisfaction.

I hope organizations will help employees understand their purpose. Simply mapping out how each job contributes to the overall product or service is a good start. Then, adding why the service or product is important to customers completes the understanding. Taking time to share it with employees can go a long way.

There are additional actions that can make this even more impactful. Sharing good customer feedback helps employees feel appreciated for their purpose. Involving employees in improving their work shows its importance to customers. And, if feasible, giving employees a chance to interact with customers directly can build connections.

Involvement: How We Work Together

Integral to *Real*ationship-Driven Cultures is the concept of employee Involvement, specifically Involvement in running the business. When employees are not just participants but co-creators in the business, a remarkable shift occurs. They move from being passive cogs in the machine to active architects of their organizational experience. This Involvement is not a mere allocation of tasks; it is an invitation to contribute, innovate, and impact. Through Involvement, employees find self-worth by making significant contributions.

Involvement must be real. It should not be a check-the-inclusion box exercise. This is a practical and impactful place to use the Mindset we covered earlier: Actions Enhance Words. The right employees should be involved in a meaningful way. Organizations must systematically and frequently involve employees in running the business.

One example of taking involvement to the next level happened during my time as Head of Talent Management. My CHRO had an idea to leverage our Employee Resources Groups (ERGs) more strategically. We created an Affinity Board, which consisted of a couple members from each of the ERGs as well as a few additional employees interested in having a strategic impact by leveraging talent management to create an environment where everyone was excited to be part of. The Affinity Board acted as my "Board of Directors." I involved them in things like creating talent strategies, developing curriculum, and prioritizing talent solutions.

The idea turned out to be a great success. Affinity Board members made meaningful contributions through their diverse backgrounds and experiences. Our talent function benefited from their ideas. We were able to provide talent solutions that were well thought out and were in sync with what the organization needed. The impact was meaningful and inspiring.

Obviously, not everyone can be involved in any given project or block of work, but involving more employees brings additional ideas, opinions, skills, and talents. If we leverage that contribution effectively, we will have better outcomes. As people come together to do the work, they feel valued because they are valuable.

Involvement includes four dimensions that impact Self-worth. It's more than just including employees in superficial ways; it requires Involvement in running the business in a meaningful way.

The Involvement Environmental Element is made up of four pillars:

- Strategic Collaboration
- Impactful Decision Making
- Meaningful Contributions
- Accountability

Strategic Collaboration

Strategic collaboration is a critical element in getting employees involved in running the business. Using a strategic approach, we can ensure that we don't collaborate for collaboration's sake. Every meeting should have an impact on the work of the business in a meaningful way. When meetings are impactful, they are another way that employees are involved in running the business.

You may remember that collaboration shows up in the Leader-to-Employee *Real*ationship. It sets the expectation that the leader will encourage, support, and act regarding collaboration. It is the leader's responsibility to make sure it happens, and it is done well.

The role of the Company-to-Employee *Real*ationship in collaboration is systems and processes. Tools increase the performance and results of collaboration. By making collaboration easier, employees are less likely to waste time and more likely to have a positive experience collaborating with coworkers.

Collaboration as part of the Environmental Element of Involvement makes collaboration a cultural expectation. It creates a broader group of employees in running the business. The benefit to the individual is increased self-worth. They are adding value to their coworkers and the company. The company benefits from more diverse views, ideas, and solutions.

Studies show that the results of a team significantly outperform the results of the individual. In the *Harvard Business Review* article "Collaborative Overload," authors Rob Cross, Reb Rebele, and Adam Grant discuss the unintended consequences of excessive collaboration within organizations.[69] They highlight that while collaboration is essential, it can lead to overburdening certain employees, diminishing productivity, and causing burnout. In my opinion, these unintended consequences are a result of not doing collaboration well, not the act of collaborating. The article identifies several key pitfalls:

1. **Over-Reliance on a Few Individuals:** Organizations often depend heavily on a select group of employees for collaborative efforts, leading to their overwork and potential burnout.

2. **Inefficient Use of Time:** Excessive meetings and communications can consume significant time, reducing the capacity for focused, individual work.

3. **Diffusion of Responsibility:** In collaborative settings, accountability can become diluted, leading to decreased ownership and initiative among team members.

4. **Decision-Making Bottlenecks:** Requiring consensus in collaborations can slow down decision-making processes, hindering agility and responsiveness.

To address these challenges and foster strategic collaboration, organizations can implement the following practices:

1. **Diversify Collaborative Roles:** Over-relying on a few individuals typically happens because each area of expertise, like finance, engineering, and supply chain, among others, has a person who stands out as having the best people skills and the most technical knowledge. That person ends up being the one to represent that area of expertise for every collaboration opportunity.

Avoid overburdening the same individuals by distributing collaborative opportunities across a broader group. This approach not only prevents burnout but also leverages diverse perspectives and skills. We could use the collaboration opportunity to build people skills for a different employee from that same area.

Not all collaboration requires the same level of expertise. Consider what level of expertise is needed for a given collaboration opportunity. Maybe a lower level of technical expertise is all you need. This different way of looking at who will be involved on a case-by-case basis can spread the collaboration across multiple employees, reducing the time commitment for each individual.

2. **Establish Clear Objectives and Boundaries:** Define the purpose and scope of collaborative efforts to ensure they are goal-oriented and time-efficient. Setting clear expectations helps maintain focus and prevents unnecessary meetings.

    In my experience, many organizations have too many meetings. Employees are generally quick to add meetings and slow to cancel them, resulting in an increase in meetings over time. So, when a meeting to collaborate is added, it is mostly met with resistance.

    Ineffective meetings are the root cause of employees' disinterest in meetings. If meetings are valuable, employees are generally happy to attend. The rules for making collaboration meetings effective are the same as for any other meeting.

Start by highly scrutinizing invite lists. Employees should not be invited just to make them feel included or to not hurt their feelings. There are plenty of opportunities to get employees involved in a meaningful way. Make sure everyone invited can either add value or receive value. Those who do both are likely the main participants. If someone only adds or receives value, ask if they need to be there for the entire meeting. If yes, include them. If not, invite them for a specific time in the meeting. If you unemotionally do this evaluation for all your meetings, the number of meetings will go down. Doing this for all meetings moving forward will ensure that meetings are productive.

A few other best practices to keep meetings effective include having an agenda, ensuring participation, practicing good time management, and making sure to have follow-up with accountability.

- A well-prepared agenda provides a roadmap for the meeting, outlines the topics to be discussed, and allocates time for each item. Share the agenda in advance to allow participants to prepare.
- Foster a collaborative environment to encourage active involvement from all attendees. Use open-ended questions and assign roles, such as timekeeper or note-taker, to ensure engagement and accountability. A collaborative meeting will make participants feel valued, expand information, and increase decision-making quality.

- Start and end on schedule to respect everyone's time. Stick to the agenda and avoid tangents to maintain focus and productivity.
- Summarize decisions and assign clear action items with deadlines. Promptly share meeting minutes to keep everyone aligned and accountable for the next steps.

3. **Promote Accountability:** Assign specific roles and responsibilities within collaborative projects to ensure clarity and ownership. This practice encourages individual initiative and reduces the diffusion of responsibility. Providing clarity regarding accountability is done best proactively. Understanding who will do what avoids confusion, delays, and unnecessary conflict. If you wait until you have accountability issues to provide clarity, you will likely increase conflict and create a sense of making it up as you go. The person who owns it after the fact will likely feel blamed and resent not knowing in advance that they were responsible.

4. **Streamline Decision-making Processes:** Implement decision-making frameworks that balance the need for input with the necessity for timely action. Empowering individuals or small teams to make decisions within defined parameters can enhance efficiency.

   Like accountability, decision-making processes should be well-defined ahead of time. Knowing who and how decisions will be made sets clear expectations. Knowing the decision process reduces conflict and improves decision efficiency and effectiveness.

By adopting these strategies, organizations can harness the benefits of collaboration while mitigating its potential drawbacks, leading to more effective and sustainable collaboration and teamwork. Over the years, I have seen a tendency in organizations to abandon tools and processes that don't work without asking the appropriate questions. Before abandoning a tool ask:

- Did we use the tool consistently?
- Did we use the tool as intended?
- Did we explore adapting the tool to our context?

Asking these questions before we stop using a tool ensures that it isn't "operator error" preventing the tool from working. Using good strategy and planning, we can increase innovation, creativity, and involvement through Strategic Collaboration.

Impactful Decision Making

Another way to Enrich Self-worth through Involvement in running the business is decision-making. Being involved in meaningful decisions is a source of impact and satisfaction for employees. When employees make decisions, it increases their impact. The benefits of getting more people involved in decisions go beyond employee satisfaction. Studies show that group decision-making outperforms even the highest-performing individual in that same group.

As stated in the Strategic Collaboration section, defining decision-making processes proactively creates clear expectations and reduces conflict caused by being surprised about our role in a particular decision. Companies can have a general approach to decision-making and even identify what types of decisions will be made with the different types of decisions. Because not all decisions can be pre-identified, it is important for leaders to clearly state what type of decision will be made in specific situations.

There are some general decision types to consider. It is important to get clarity prior to decision time to eliminate surprises. The first step is to identify what decision types you will use. Then, create clear definitions and rules for each decision type. Developing and documenting general rules around overall philosophy and when each decision type is used increases understanding. Finally, the decision types and approaches must be communicated. Plan to communicate more than once and have feedback mechanisms to bring the decision strategy to life.

Some recommended decision types and uses are listed here and are a good place to start. The leader decides on their own. In a few situations, this is best. Having a culture of getting employees involved in decision-making should not morph into everybody being involved in every decision. The leader/employee should decide on their own if the timing doesn't allow input, it is an emergency, the decision impact is low, or it is routine. For situations where the leader wants to control the outcome, they may want to seek input yet retain the right to make the final decision.

Yes, even I think we should have this on our list of decision types. Of course, I caution leaders not to overuse it. Remember, although you involve others, the level of involvement is reduced. This method is best used when the leader has most of the information. As a leader, you will have access to different information and be in different meetings than your team. If the decision requires information that your team doesn't have but you want their unique perspective, getting input from your team and making the final decision is best.

The final decision method is the team deciding. For this method, the leader has input and decision authority equal to the team. In many situations, this can be pretty smooth. The team works out the best decision based on input from everyone. Even if not all team members completely agree, they are willing to move forward with the majority of the team. For cases where there may be resistance to moving forward, it is best to have already built out rules for getting past a deadlock.

It is important to understand the deadline for making the decision. You can't let it drag out at the expense of the project or work. After hearing out all sides of the debate, check to see what decision each team member would make. From this, you will likely get a sense of the direction the team wants to go. It is not a simple vote where the majority wins, but as the deadline nears and everyone has been heard, taking the direction of the majority is the right thing to do.

Strong leaders excel in team decision-making, while conflict-avoidant and indecisive leaders tend to struggle. Leaders who want to please everyone fail miserably. To be successful, you must set and maintain clear expectations. If the team stalls, you must take action and hold the team accountable for making timely decisions.

Getting more employees involved in meaningful decisions enriches their self-worth and increases decision quality.

Meaningful Contributions

Employees who feel their work is valued and impactful are more engaged, motivated, and committed to the organization. By creating an environment where contributions are recognized as meaningful, you can foster a deeper sense of ownership, purpose, and connection among employees.

Sometimes, employees forget or don't understand the value of their work. Regularly acknowledge the value and impact of employees' contributions, emphasizing their importance to the team and the company's success. When they are appreciated, employees are willing to increase their involvement. Recognition comes in various forms, ranging from a simple but specific thank you to a formal celebration. Some companies have formal recognition programs. The most important thing is to recognize employees regularly to make them feel that their contributions matter.

Through opportunities for growth, you provide chances for employees to stretch their skills and take on projects that align with their strengths and aspirations. As employees gain new skills and increase their contribution, their work holds more meaning. Development assignments are a great way to increase an employee's self-worth while making the organization more successful.

We show trust in employees to do their own work and make decisions, showing that their input is valued through empowerment. All jobs in every organization have meaning. Leaders who empower employees create more opportunities for them to make meaningful contributions and enrich their self-worth.

Find ways to involve employees in the strategy. Participating in the company's direction gives them meaning, and the strategy benefits from additional perspectives and input. Also, invite employees to participate in discussions about goals and projects so they feel they are shaping and implementing organizational strategy.

Leaders can highlight the outcomes of an employee's work during feedback sessions, linking it to broader objectives. Feedback is a great, versatile tool. In this case, it can be used to highlight the important work employees are doing. Be sure to include the impact of work and special accomplishments.

Share examples of how employees' work has positively impacted the organization, customers, or community. Through stories, leaders can show the impact of employees' work from the perspective of others. Customer feedback and letters from the community are great ways to connect employees to the impact of their work.

Accountability

If you want a culture of getting results, it starts with account-ability. Accountability impacts everything you do, including safety, performance, continuous improvement, goals, and objectives. For accountability to thrive, you must remove the negative perception many employees have.

Accountability starts with setting clear expectations. Two tools can help to create clarity: SMART goals and RACI. SMART (Specific, Measurable, Attainable, Relevant, and Timely) goals have been around for a while and are typ-ically used in performance management processes. They can add clarity outside of performance management, including work assignments and projects. By answering each of these elements, you have enough detail to create clarity.

Another way to create clarity is to define roles and responsibilities. A great tool to use is the RACI (Responsible, Accountable, Consult, and Inform) method. Basically, it assigns different levels of responsibility by going beyond who "owns" a task. This level of clarity gets everyone on the same page. You can easily find information and templates on both tools online.

There are multiple theories regarding who should drive accountability. Some argue it resides with the individual, some promote holding each other accountable, and some say the leaders own accountability. I believe accountability should be a team sport and recommend leveraging all three.

Accountability works best as a team sport. Three sources of accountability create the best results. Holding ourselves accountable should be the foundation. Holding each other accountable should augment accountability. Our relationship should allow us to challenge each other. The leader should also be involved with accountability. However, over-reliance on the leader is not a good idea. The leader should create the environment where accountability is welcome and step in only occasionally in specific situations.

Individuals should learn to embrace getting things done and keeping commitments. They should be open to feedback and welcome reminders. For teams, we should expect strong relationships open to holding each other accountable. Teams that hold each other accountable prevent the leader from being in the middle of accountability for everything. We should hold each other accountable with good intentions. It should come from a place of caring, and focus on getting results. The leader should play an important role in accountability. By creating a culture of accountability, the leader sets the tone that accountability is what we do here. Additionally, the leader may have to step in sometimes to provide reminders, create understanding, and reset expectations.

Good interpersonal skills can positively impact accountability. Good communication skills pave the way for positive interactions when addressing accountability issues. Emotional intelligence allows you to recognize and deal with sensitivity and conflict regarding accountability.

Good time management has a huge impact on your ability to get things done. Ongoing feedback helps address issues when they are more manageable.

Service: How We Win Together

Service, the act of adding value to others, emerges as a natural extension of strong relationships and living our deepest purpose: relationships. In serving, we transcend our individual concerns and connect with others in meaningful ways. This Service Mindset is not about subservience; it is about empowerment. It is through serving that we find our place in the organization, adding our unique talents to the larger mission. Greater good behavior increases our ability to win and drive organizational success.

Service starts by focusing on the greater good. Instead of focusing on winning for ourselves, we choose actions and make decisions that benefit the team, function, and overall company. Service is such a critical element of *Real*ationship-Driven Cultures that it shows up in the Five Mindsets, in *Real*ationship purposes, and as one of the Four Environmental Elements.

Service is the best antidote for the most detrimental behavior in organizational life: self-serving employees. You may notice that service also shows up in the Employee-to-Employee *Real*ationship as one of its purposes. Additionally, it is one of the Five Mindsets. This full-court press on service is a key concept in accomplishing a culture of service.

Conformity theory shows that people will change their behavior to fit in with the group. So, we embed service in the way we think (Mindset), our purpose for interaction (Employee-to-Employee *Real*ationship), and as an

Environment Element. By using three methods of promoting Service, we are more likely to make it part of the culture. As we get more employees to serve the greater good, it becomes more likely that others will do the same.

Service is critical to a healthy organizational culture. It builds trust and strong work relationships, creating enjoyment and engagement in our work. It creates self-worth when employees serve each other and the organization. When employees have a positive impact on the organization, they feel valued.

Greater Good = Company, Function, Team, Self

In a work environment, the foundation of serving others is to think about the greater good. Employees should strive to add value to the team, function, and company. It is easy for employees to get caught up in looking for their next promotion. When promotion becomes the primary focus, decisions and actions are based on what benefits the individual, not the greater good. Selfish behavior is extremely disruptive. It weakens relationships, increases water cooler complaint time, and creates misguided competitiveness.

Selfish behaviors can survive for a few reasons. In a toxic culture, selfish behaviors run rampant. They become a way of life and consist of a never-ending series of moves and countermoves. Competition is focused on beating each other to the top of the corporate ladder, with little focus on beating the competition.

Even in otherwise good cultures, selfish behavior can exist. If the self-server controls the narrative, they make it seem like everyone else is the problem and they are the hero trying to fix it. At a minimum, the self-server creates the illusion of productivity, making it less likely that they will be challenged. In some cases, the self-server accomplishes many individual goals, but the overall company result is not what it could be. Additionally, self-serving behaviors may exist because others may not speak up. They may not want to rock the boat. They may fear that they will be viewed as the problem.

Serving Gives Us Value

For employees to build Self-worth through Service, companies must create environments where service holds more value than self-serving behaviors. Individual self-worth is deeper and more lasting when it comes from serving others and the greater good. However, if the workplace environment ignores or encourages self-serving behaviors, conformity theory ensures that you will have a culture of people looking out for their own benefit instead of serving the greater good.

Through talent processes and leadership accountability, companies can reinforce a mindset and behaviors of service. When employees are focused on serving the greater good, everyone benefits. Serving others is selfless and brings the individual satisfaction and self-worth.

Although the Environmental Element of Service's main purpose is to create Self-worth, it also impacts Unity. When we put others first, we also create connection and unity. Others appreciate selfless acts. This builds trust and creates a caring environment—employees like being involved in an environment that prioritizes the greater good. When everyone focuses on supporting the company, function, and team, the chances of success increase greatly.

Personal Characteristics

Personal characteristics and approaches lay the foundation to get fulfillment from serving. Although these characteristics come more naturally to some people, they are definitely a choice. We can decide to approach life according to these noble character choices. Some of us may have to work at it until these become more natural, but we can all choose to live based on these principles if we want to.

Humility

To achieve a life of service, we must first humble ourselves. If you remember, the most detrimental behaviors to work relationships and company performance are self-serving behaviors. If we are going to eliminate self-serving behaviors, we have to get employees focused on serving each other and the overall company. It is better to focus on the behavior you want to add than the behavior you want to eliminate. It is more positive and creates more conversations about what is wanted, which will be more effective. For this reason, the *Real*ationship-Driven approach focuses on what we want to move toward.

Humility is central to accomplishing an environment of service. The more we realize we are part of something bigger, the more we can put our own needs aside for the greater good. Without humility, it is easy to focus on our needs and how to get ahead individually. Our thoughts and actions become habitual. The more we strive for our own needs at the expense of others, the easier it is to continue that path.

When everyone has humility, it refocuses our definition of competition. We start competing for the greater good and not for our own promotions. This frees us to serve others and the company. The good news is that as we all operate with humility, we each get credit for our good work. Interestingly, it comes from others bragging about us, not us bragging about ourselves. We are happy to see our colleagues succeed and celebrate their victories and promotions. These collective efforts benefit the overall performance of the company, which drives continued growth and success.

Gratitude

Gratitude is important to our wellbeing. Studies show that people who are grateful are happier and less stressed. When we are grateful and acknowledge it, we are more likely to be of service to others and build strong relationships. Being grateful for what we have increases our ability to not strive for more at all costs. Gratitude gives us the freedom to help others succeed.

It can be difficult to have gratitude. Human brains are designed for survival, so we tend to hold on to negative information. This is extremely beneficial in life-threatening situations. Unfortunately, it is easy to hold on to negative information and feedback, even if it is not pertinent to our survival. With this strong natural tendency to focus on the negative, it is easy to lose sight of what we have to be grateful for.

It is good to add gratitude into your life. There are many ways to ensure being grateful is part of your life. Keeping a gratitude journal helps us consider the good things happening in our lives. Referencing the journal refreshes our memory of the great stuff happening in our lives. You can start team meetings at work with each member sharing something they are grateful for. It can be work-related or personal. Leaders can share what they are grateful for in each of their team members. You can do it in team meetings and during one-on-one meetings. Sharing what you appreciate about your employees reminds them of their positive contributions to the team and company and ensures they know you are noticing their good work.

Gratitude helps us have a positive mindset. When we are positive, we are better learners, better problem solvers, and more resilient. The benefits of gratitude are well documented, yet most people don't focus on it. When I ask people to share something they are grateful for, many times, they struggle to find something to share. Eventually, they typically do, but it usually takes a little effort. Building your own gratefulness, helping others be more grateful, and sharing what you're thankful for with others increases positivity and improves our work environment.

Empathy

Empathy is the ability to understand and share the feelings of others. Empathy for others increases connection. It is a critical element of emotional intelligence and our human condition. We all have a strong need to be understood.

Empathy doesn't require you to agree with the emotions someone else is feeling in a particular situation. Instead, it's about recognizing and connecting with the emotion itself. Here's an example to illustrate this point.

Imagine someone is cut off in traffic. For one person, this might lead to frustration and irritation. Another person, however, might not feel frustrated at all. Despite the different reactions, empathy allows us to connect because we've all experienced both frustration and the act of being cut off in traffic at some point in our lives.

The underlying emotion is likely familiar even if the exact circumstances don't resonate with you. You can use that shared emotional experience to connect with the other person's feelings, even if you wouldn't react the same way in their situation. This is the beauty of empathy; it's not about judging whether the other person's emotions are right or wrong or whether you would feel the same way. It's about meeting them where they are and sharing in the experience of being human.

Empathy is a skill; like any skill, it can be developed with intentional practice. To build stronger connections and better understand the emotions of others, you can practice and implement skills that make you more empathetic. Active listening is the beginning of empathy. You must truly hear what is being shared and any emotions that go along with it. Using open-ended questions increases active listening and uncovers more information relevant to the discussion. By remembering when you felt a similar emotion, you can connect on a deeper level. Don't judge. Set aside your temptation to assume they should respond similarly to you. Take time to imagine what it's like to be in their situation. What pressures, fears, or hopes might they be experiencing?

Building empathy requires practice and intentionality, but the rewards are worth it. We can practice empathy at work, at home, and with strangers. Empathy strengthens relationships, builds trust, and creates environments where people feel seen and valued. When we make empathy a habit, we connect with others and create a culture of understanding which benefits everyone.

Richard Boyatzis and Annie McKee point out the importance of resonance. They state, "Resonance enables the leader to use this expertise in pursuit of the company's performance. It allows the leader to engage the power of all

of the people who work in and around the organization."[70]
When we are overly stressed, it typically hinders our ability to build and maintain relationships and serve others. *Real*ationship-Driven Cultures go a long way to reduce the overall stress of navigating the work environment. As a way of amplifying the benefits of a reduced stress environment, the renewal processes shared in *Resonant Leadership* help us be our best.

PART 3

OUTCOMES AND HOW TO GET THERE

Three Outcomes

```
┌─────────────────────────────────────────────────────────────┐
│                                                               │
│   ( 3 OUTCOMES ───────────────────────────────────────●      │
│                                                               │
│        1. Unity                                               │
│        2. Self-worth                                          │
│        3. Resilience                                          │
│        (Unity and Self-worth create Resilience)               │
│                                                               │
└─────────────────────────────────────────────────────────────┘
```

Throughout this book, we have explored the challenges facing workplace relationships and the transformative power of *Real*ationship-Driven Cultures. We've examined the

Foundational Beliefs, Key Organizational *Real*ationships, and the Environmental Elements that influence how people connect and work together.

We will now explore in more detail our primary Outcomes Unity, Self-worth, and Resilience. When relationships are prioritized, the workplace becomes more than a place to complete tasks; it becomes a community where people feel a sense of belonging, purpose, and shared success. This transformation creates Resilience and workplaces that employees seek.

Resilience allows organizations and individuals to navigate challenges, adapt to change, and remain strong in the face of adversity. These are not abstract ideals. They are tangible, measurable results that emerge when relationships are intentionally strengthened.

Finally, we'll explore the Path Forward. For organizations seeking to implement *Real*ationship-Driven Cultures, this final chapter outlines how to take the next steps, whether through internal initiatives or with expert guidance. I'll share insights into how my consulting and executive search work helps organizations build cultures that not only attract and retain top talent but also create environments where people and businesses thrive.

Strong relationships are not just a means to an end. *Real*ationships are the foundation of long-term success. When organizations commit to Fostering Unity, Enriching Self-worth, and Building Resilience, they create workplaces where people don't just show up to work, they show up for each other.

CHAPTER 9

OUTCOMES

All Four Environmental Elements play a role in all Three Outcomes: Unity, Self-worth, and Resilience. However, some of the elements have a bigger impact on specific outcomes than others. While it's not critical to know which elements directly impact which outcomes, I will cover it for deeper understanding and your ability to impact your environment.

Three Outcomes

The results of a *Real*ationship-Driven Culture are three significant outcomes. Starting with the Three Foundational Beliefs, creating clarity on Organizational *Real*ationships, and using Focused Talent Management to impact the Four Environmental Elements, we Foster Unity, Enrich Self-worth, and Build Resilience.

Implementing *Real*ationship-Driven Cultures helps us move toward positive behaviors and positive outcomes. Although our goal is to stop self-serving behaviors, reverse division, and discourage burnout, we focus our efforts on what we want to work toward: Unity, Self-worth, and Resilience. In talent management, leadership, and culture work, the focus often defaults to what needs to stop. But stopping something is not the same as creating something better. That's why the core Outcomes of a *Real*ationship-Driven Cultures are not just solutions to workplace struggles; they are the foundation of an environment where people want to work, contribute, and grow.

Shifting our focus toward what we want to achieve changes everything. Instead of trying to manage dysfunction, we build strength. Instead of policing behaviors, we create purpose. When leaders make Unity, Self-worth, and Resilience the center of their culture, the need for excessive control and correction fades. People naturally align with environments that support them, making division, self-interest, and exhaustion less viable in the first place. This book is about that shift, not just fixing workplace issues, but creating something far more powerful. A culture that thrives because of the relationships within it.

Having a positive attitude allows us to fully commit and more effectively focus on the Beliefs, *Real*ationships, and Environmental Elements. The Outcomes come as a result of that commitment and focus. The outcomes are a result of creating the right environment that drives a positive, strong culture. The positive focus creates more energy and passion and drives us toward the outcomes, so it is better to focus on the things we need to do to achieve the desired outcomes.

When I was young, I went to a small high school in South Central, PA. We had a terrible track record in football. We were lucky to win two games a season, so the school hired a new coach to try to improve the program. One of the changes he implemented was changing our focus on winning. He set the tone early on that we would not talk much about winning. We talked a lot about what it took to become a winning program, like discipline, hard work, practice, and dedication. In fact, after our very first scrimmage, he admonished us for raising our index finger to make the number one sign. He told us we had not earned the right to say we were number one, and our focus should not be on winning and being number one. Instead, he wanted us to focus on the things it took to be number one and make sure our actions and follow-through supported it. In the end, he turned the program around. Despite being the smallest school in the area, we won the school's first football championship.

Although our Three Outcomes (Unity, Self-Worth, Resilience) are why we implement *Rea*lationship-Driven Cultures, the work lies in what we do. When we fully commit to the actions (Beliefs, *Rea*lationships, and Environmental Elements) it takes to reach our goals, it increases our chances of success. For example, one of our goals is Unity. We need to know what actions it takes to create Unity. If we only talk about and hope for unity, we are not likely to achieve it. Our time is better spent thinking about and acting on what it takes to achieve unity.

Unity: In It Together

Unity is a key outcome of building a *Rea*lationship-Driven Culture. Webster's Dictionary defines unity in multiple ways.

1. "the quality or state of not being multiple: ONENESS"
2. "a condition of harmony: ACCORD"
3. "a totality of related parts: an entity that is a complex or systematic whole"

These definitions provide the essence of unity created by a *Real*ationship-Driven Culture.

*Real*ationship-Driven Cultures create an atmosphere of being in it together and strive for Unity through deep connection. The goal is to go beyond just being willing to work with each other. There is a sincere effort to help others be successful. When our coworkers succeed, it brings us joy. We look forward to working together, overcoming obstacles collaboratively, and accomplishing company goals. We value fulfilling common purposes together. We derive meaning from the company's purpose and working together.

Our Five Mindsets and Multi-level Purpose unify employees. Using the principles of Five Mindsets, you can create stronger *Real*ationships based on mutual respect and benefit. As we positively live out our deepest purpose of relationships, we are unified with others. In organizational life, employees are unified in creating success for each other and the company through healthy relationships. Multi-level Purposes further unify employees through connections that go beyond team goals.

Mindsets are the thoughts that guide our interactions with others. They can strengthen our relationships in a way that unites us and brings us together. Since our actions typically follow our mindsets, the way we think is paramount to strong, positive relationships. Mindsets create relationships that are strong, productive, and united when positive, constructive thoughts guide us.

Purpose is another Key Environmental Element of *Real*ationships. I believe Purpose is multi-level. The levels include our most important purpose of being in relationships, as well as our life's purpose, and the purpose we serve in our company and job. Additionally, each of the Four *Real*ationships has four purposes. By adding purpose to relationships, we focus on what is important to advancing the relationship and making it meaningful.

Serving Purpose with others is very unifying. It brings people together to focus on a common pursuit. Of course, successfully fulfilling Purpose is both gratifying and unifying. But, even when we face obstacles and struggles in pursuing goals, we can be united with those we work with.

When employees connect through Purpose, they focus on bigger, higher-impact pursuits. As the importance and impact rise in what we are working on, our unity strengthens. Additionally, when we live out our purposes, we are more motivated, positive, calm, and less stressed. These emotions pave the way to stronger relationships. It is easier to resolve differences, overcome challenges, and prioritize the relationship.

Unity creates a commitment to each other and the company. Employees invest in the success of everyone within the company. This investment creates synergy and alignment focused on making the organization successful. Suddenly, employees aren't doing a job. They are playing a role in helping coworkers and the company be successful, providing great customer experiences, and creating exceptional products and services. Customers are not viewed as a transaction to support the company. They are viewed as someone to be in a relationship with and care about. Customers' needs and relationships are prioritized and viewed as more important than the money exchanged for products and services.

Self-Worth: Feel Valued by Adding Value to Others

*Real*ationship-Driven Cultures also create an atmosphere of Self-worth. Employees feel valued by adding value to the business and their fellow employees. When employees impact the business through meaningful work, decision making, and collaboration, they feel valued, which gives them a sense of Self-worth. Through Service and serving the greater good, we help others be successful and create collective success. We impact others when we help them succeed, which in turn increases our Self-worth.

As humans, we have a strong need to be valued and want our lives to mean something. Self-worth is created in two ways. First is Involvement. When employees are involved and contribute to the results of the company, they feel valued. Their contributions matter. The second driver of Self-worth is Service. Employees add value to all work relationships, as well as their team, function, and company. When we add value, we feel valued.

Strategic collaboration sets the stage for sharing expertise on cross-functional projects and work. Sharing information and perspectives leverages employees' expertise. A holistic approach improves outcomes and decisions, and employees' self-worth increases when they share their skills and knowledge.

Making meaningful decisions provides value, which creates self-worth. It positively impacts the company if a good decision is made. It negatively impacts the business if a bad decision is made. Regardless, the fact that the decision will have an impact makes it valuable to feel involved.

Further, if a bad decision is made, it is an opportunity for employees to learn. Learning is beneficial to the individual and the company. Although Self-worth is the dominant outcome of Involvement, Unity is also impacted. When employees work together, collaborate to overcome obstacles, and collectively solve problems, it strengthens connections.

Accountability creates trust and improves results. Creating a culture of accountability is crucial to strong, positive relationships. We need to rely on each other to do our part, or raise any issues preventing us from doing it.

A culture of service also creates self-worth. Serving others is likely the most valuable thing we can do. It builds gratitude and connection, strengthening relationships. You get a sense of accomplishment when you help others succeed. *Real*ationship-Driven Cultures create an environment where service is the norm. Everyone supports each other and focuses on serving the greater good. The collective success created is broader, longer lasting, and more satisfying.

We encourage service by creating an environment where it is expected and rewarded. When service becomes a way of life, employees realize intrinsic and extrinsic benefits. Intrinsically, most people get a good feeling when they are part of something bigger than themselves and contribute to collective success. Extrinsically, when the organization's talent processes and systems reward service, employees who serve receive more promotions, raises, and bonuses.

Resilience: Effort Is Worth It

In 2024, resilience has become a focal point for organizations as they strive to create sustainable cultures that can withstand ongoing challenges. One in five employees globally has left their jobs due to poor company culture, emphasizing the need for organizations to build stronger cultural foundations rather than relying on surface-level perks or temporary solutions. Companies increasingly focus on aligning their core values and strategies with long-term resilience to attract and retain talent.[71]

When employees are united with each other and feel valued, they are much more resilient. Unity, or connection to each other, builds commitment to our relationships. This tie makes it easier to see the good in others, minimizes negative reactions to idiosyncrasies, and increases our enjoyment of spending time with each other. Strong connections to others make our interactions less stressful. If we do encounter conflict, it is easier to resolve because our desire, confidence, and ability to resolve it are high.

The state of employee mental health in today's workplace highlights a critical need for organizations to address burnout and foster resilience.[72] According to SHRM's 2024 research, 44 percent of U.S. employees feel burned out at work, and nearly one-third often feel stressed. However, the study also reveals a powerful insight: relationships with coworkers and managers have a more significant impact on mental health than the job itself. This underscores the importance of creating cultures centered on relationships, which is the foundation of *Real*ationship-Driven Cultures.

Resilience, defined as the ability to recover from challenges and adapt to stress, is not just an individual trait; it is a collective outcome of strong relationships in the workplace. SHRM's findings show that workers who feel a strong sense of belonging are 2.5 times less likely to feel burned out. Belonging comes from environments where coworkers and managers foster connection, trust, and mutual support. When people experience relational support at work, their ability to persevere through difficulties grows, making

Resilience a direct result of the Unity and Self-worth fostered by *Real*ationship-Driven Cultures.

Unity and Self-Worth: Building the Core of Resilience

Unity, one of the Three Outcomes of *Real*ationship-Driven Cultures, emphasizes positive relationship Mindsets, shared goals, and purpose. This shared sense of purpose builds connection among employees, reducing the isolation that contributes to burnout. SHRM's study supports this, showing that 48 percent of workers say their manager has a positive impact on their mental health, highlighting the role of leadership in Fostering Unity.

Self-worth, another key outcome of *Real*ationship-Driven Cultures, focuses on employees' value and recognition within the organization. Workers who feel appreciated and supported by their managers and peers are more likely to thrive, even under pressure. In fact, SHRM data indicates that 37 percent of employees view their manager's influence as critical to their mental health, reinforcing that resilient teams stem from environments where individuals feel valued and understand the importance of team accomplishments over individual gains. Together, Unity and Self-worth create the foundation for Resilience by promoting a workplace culture where employees feel both supported and empowered.

The Business Case for *Real*ationship-Driven Cultures

The benefits of building resilience through strong workplace relationships extend beyond individual well-being—they directly impact organizational success. According to SHRM, employees experiencing burnout are nearly three times more likely to actively search for another job. This turnover costs companies billions annually in lost productivity and replacement expenses. Conversely, organizations that prioritize relationships see higher engagement, retention, and fulfillment, creating a competitive advantage in today's challenging labor market.

Moreover, resilience has a cascading effect on business outcomes. Resilient teams respond more effectively to challenges, innovate under pressure, and maintain higher levels of performance. When organizations intentionally cultivate *Real*ationship-Driven Cultures, they mitigate burnout, improve morale, and unlock the full potential of their workforce.

*Real*ationships Matter More Than the Job Itself

Perhaps the most striking insight from SHRM's study is that coworker and manager relationships have a greater influence on mental health than the job itself. While the work itself plays a role, the quality of relationships determines whether employees feel connected, supported, and motivated. *Real*ationship-Driven Cultures recognize this reality by placing relationships at the center of organizational culture and strategy.

By Fostering Unity, enriching Self-worth, and building Resilience, *Real*ationship-Driven Cultures not only enhance the employee experience but also deliver measurable business results. As this research demonstrates, investing in relationships is not just a moral imperative—it's a strategic necessity for organizations that aim to thrive in today's dynamic world.

Relational Pillars: Additional Outcomes

Our primary outcomes (Unity and Self-worth) from *Real*ationship-Driven Cultures provide additional benefits that strengthen relationships. The following Relational Pillars are needed to have strong, positive relationships.

1. Trust
2. Respect
3. Mutual Benefit
4. Empathy
5. Consistency
6. Communication

There are additional things that impact relationships; however, these six carry the most impact on the health of our relationships.

These Relational Pillars are not something we work on directly. They are the result of our behaviors. To use our terminology, they are Outcomes. Although other mindsets, behaviors, and actions impact these Relational Pillars, *Real*ationship-Driven Cultures go a long way to building these critical relationship pillars. It is beneficial to understand what these Relational Pillars are, their impact on relationships, and how *Real*ationship-Driven Cultures impact them.

Trust

Trust is the belief in the reliability, integrity, and competence of others. Studies show that trust forms the basis of social capital, allowing people to work effectively and cooperate, even in challenging environments.[73] [74] Trust is linked to higher psychological safety, which enhances collaboration and performance.[75] Without trust, teams often struggle with vulnerability and openness, which are essential for innovation and meaningful collaboration.

Strategic Collaboration and Accountability reside within the Environmental Element we call Involvement. This element shapes how we contribute to the success of the organization. Through our daily work, we gain opportunities to reinforce our reliability, integrity, and competence. Each time we follow through on our promises, prioritize the organization's goals, and treat our colleagues with respect, we add trust.

In an organization where employees collaborate meaningfully, they share their expertise and experiences, enriching their team and the organization as a whole. When employees collaborate effectively, they don't just complete tasks; they exchange knowledge, share perspectives, and collectively solve problems. This shared expertise enriches the organization and strengthens individual capabilities, allowing everyone to contribute to a broader purpose.

When we leverage our unique skills to run the business, we not only validate our competence but also reinforce trust in our abilities. By consistently meeting commitments and holding ourselves accountable, we increase our reliability and integrity. And as trust deepens, so does unity across the organization.

Moreover, accountability serves as a powerful trust-building tool. When we deliver on our commitments and hold ourselves to high standards, we demonstrate reliability. By setting an example and holding ourselves responsible for outcomes, we affirm our dedication to shared goals, fostering a culture where trust is the foundation.

As trust expands, so does unity. Colleagues who trust each other can depend on one another, leading to more cohesive teamwork and a stronger sense of purpose. This alignment enables an organization to achieve more than any individual could accomplish alone.

Respect

Respect involves acknowledging others' worth, opinions, and autonomy. Respect has been shown to correlate with higher job satisfaction and organizational commitment.[76] When people feel respected, they experience greater well-being and are more likely to reciprocate respectful behavior, reinforcing positive interactions.[77] Respect fosters an environment where individuals feel valued, leading to more robust, genuine connections.

The Environmental Element of *Service* invites us to shift our focus outward, prioritizing the needs of the organization and the greater good over personal gain. By doing so, we not only demonstrate respect for our colleagues but actively contribute to a culture that values each individual. Serving others shows a willingness to elevate collective goals, underscoring that everyone's contributions matter. This commitment to service goes beyond transactional interactions; it reflects a deeper respect for the value each person brings to the organization.

A core trait that reinforces this value is *Humility*. Humility encourages us to recognize and appreciate others' worth, fostering a reciprocal environment of respect. By humbly acknowledging the strengths, perspectives, and efforts of others, we lay the groundwork for genuine connections and mutual regard. Respect flourishes in an environment where individuals feel seen and valued, creating a cycle that builds self-worth in both ourselves and our colleagues.

High respect doesn't just influence interpersonal dynamics; it also strengthens the foundation of the entire organization. When respect is present, people feel secure in expressing their ideas and taking initiative, knowing that they will be met with openness and appreciation. This atmosphere not only boosts self-worth but also cultivates collective resilience, where individuals are motivated to contribute fully, knowing their contributions are respected.

Respect is a natural outcome in an environment rooted in service and humility. It enriches the self-worth of everyone involved and fosters the unity and strength of the organization as a whole.

Mutual Benefit

Mutual benefit focuses on creating relationships where employees find value and personal growth. Relationships based on mutual benefit promote a sense of reciprocity and partnership, leading to more equitable, long-term commitments.[78] The norm of reciprocity is fundamental in social exchange theory, where mutual exchanges lead to more sustainable relationships.

In a *Real*ationship-Driven Culture, mutual benefit is cultivated through a commitment to serving the greater good and is anchored in the Environmental Element of *Purpose*. This principle is about creating relationships that add value and foster growth for everyone involved. When interactions are guided by mutual benefit, each person feels they are contributing to something greater and gaining something meaningful in return, whether it's knowledge, support, or personal development.

When individuals align with a shared purpose, they naturally move beyond self-interest to consider how their actions impact others and the organization. Purpose gives meaning to daily interactions, transforming ordinary tasks into opportunities to serve others and reinforce shared goals. Purpose driven work becomes a powerful motivator, fostering a sense of unity and partnership. As people see their contributions leading to tangible benefits for themselves and their colleagues, they become more invested in maintaining and strengthening these relationships.

Mutual benefit also fosters unity across the organization. When individuals feel their needs are met and see personal value in their contributions, they are more likely to support others, reinforce trust, and sustain collective efforts. This interdependence helps prevent the isolation that often results from overly individualistic work cultures, creating an environment where people feel they belong and are valued.

By embracing a Mindset of Service over Self-serving and rooting actions in shared Purpose, we create a culture of mutual benefit that strengthens individual relationships and builds a resilient, unified organization.

Empathy

Empathy is crucial for building rapport, enhancing emotional intelligence, and creating supportive environments.[79] Studies also reveal that empathetic leaders foster higher engagement and collaboration.[80] Empathy bridges personal divides, creating deeper understanding and connection, particularly in diverse or challenging settings.

Within a *Real*ationship-Driven Culture, empathy manifests through the Environmental Element of Service, guiding individuals to act in the best interests of others and fostering a culture centered on service. Empathy is more than a social skill; it is foundational to developing emotional intelligence, building rapport, and creating environments where people feel supported and valued.[81]

Empathy allows leaders and colleagues to approach others with understanding, not judgment, enabling constructive, inclusive, and solution-focused conversations. This trait is vital in building an environment where individuals are motivated to serve the greater good, knowing that contributions and experiences are acknowledged and respected.

Humans are wired to experience and interpret stimuli through an emotional lens before engaging in logical reasoning. This emotional processing is the brain's way of assessing threats, rewards, and social cues, setting the stage for our behaviors and interactions. Because we first interpret situations emotionally, empathy becomes essential for creating authentic connections. When people feel that others genuinely care, they are more likely to respond with openness, trust, and collaboration, creating a positive feedback loop that strengthens relationships over time.

Emotions drive behavior, and when empathy is present, people are motivated to act in ways that uplift others and promote the greater good. Empathy fosters a workplace culture where individuals aren't just colleagues but allies in each other's growth and well-being. It deepens an organization's relational foundation, making it resilient and adaptable to opportunities and challenges.

In a *Real*ationship-Driven Culture, the Environmental Element of Service creates empathy as we factor in the greater good in our actions and decisions. This approach builds bonds that go beyond mere professional interactions, cultivating a shared commitment to an environment where every person feels valued, understood, and inspired to contribute.

Consistency

Consistency involves maintaining reliable and predictable behaviors over time. It is closely linked with trust, as predictability allows individuals to feel secure in their interactions.[82] Research on attachment theory also underscores that consistent behavior promotes psychological security.[83] Consistency fosters stability in relationships, allowing people to rely on one another, even during times of change.

Consistency in relationships is fostered through two key Environmental Elements: Mindsets and Purpose. These elements create a steady foundation for consistency that reduces stress and promotes positive, rewarding interactions, allowing for stronger connections and unity within the organization.

*Real*ationship-Driven Cultures create consistency in relationships through the Five Mindsets as one of the Environmental Elements. The Mindsets set clear expectations and agreements on how employees treat each other. When our interactions with others are consistent, relationships are less stressful and are more rewarding. Feeling connection and unity come easy when our interactions with others are more relaxed and stress-free.

The Five Mindsets serve as guiding principles, setting clear expectations and agreements on how employees interact. These shared Mindsets are like a compass for behavior, giving everyone in the organization a common understanding of respectful and supportive treatment. This alignment reduces ambiguity and promotes predictability in relationships, lowering the stress often associated with inconsistent interactions. When people know what to expect from their colleagues, they can approach interactions with confidence, feeling secure in the stability of those relationships. Consistent, positive interactions build a more relaxed environment where employees are free to focus on meaningful work rather than navigating uncertain dynamics. In such an environment, a sense of connection and unity emerges naturally, as individuals feel valued and secure.

Purpose is another powerful Environmental Element that enhances consistency. A shared purpose aligns individuals and teams around common work, goals and values, creating coherence in decision-making and actions. When employees are guided by the same purpose, they develop a unified approach to assessing options, making choices, and solving challenges. This unity in purpose minimizes discrepancies in decision criteria, ensuring that everyone is working from the same playbook and creating consistency across teams and departments. As a result, employees experience fewer misunderstandings and conflicting priorities, which allows for smoother collaboration and reinforces trust throughout the organization.

Moreover, Purpose clarifies the intent and role of each of the Four Key Organizational *Real*ationships, including Employee-to-Employee, Leader-to-Employee, Leader-to-Leader, and Company-to-Employee. It provides a framework that supports consistent interactions. When individuals understand the underlying purpose of work relationships, they gain clarity on how to engage meaningfully within each relationship. This awareness fosters an environment where expectations are clear, communication is direct, and collaboration is purposeful. When everyone knows why a relationship exists and how it serves the organization, they are better equipped to interact in consistent, respectful, and supportive ways.

By integrating the Environment Elements, Mindsets, and Purpose, *Real*ationship-Driven Cultures create a stable foundation for consistent, reliable relationships essential for

Fostering Unity, reducing stress, and enhancing the overall employee experience. This stability allows employees to form strong, resilient bonds that contribute to a culture of trust, alignment, and shared success.

Communication

Open, honest communication is the foundation for sharing ideas, resolving conflicts, and maintaining connection. Effective communication is often identified as a top predictor of relationship satisfaction and longevity.[84] Research on workplace relationships finds that clear communication reduces misunderstandings and promotes a culture of transparency.[85] Consistent, honest communication builds clarity and minimizes potential friction, encouraging stronger relational bonds.

Good communication impacts both relationship bonds and business outcomes. Given the importance and frequency of communication throughout our workday, creating an environment where good communication is natural and thrives is paramount to success.

Poor communication divides and separates us and creates stress and tension, which makes it difficult to interact with others positively. When we are under stress, we are more likely to be in flight or fight mode because we are more likely to feel attacked. If we take an offensive approach, we increase the chances of putting the other person on the defensive. This back-and-forth interaction could easily spiral downward.

Effective communication brings us together and creates unity. It considers others' perspectives and prioritizes the relationship in times of opposing views. When we seek others' opinions and ideas as much as we share our own, we build trust and mutual benefit. With good communication, we are relaxed and able to explore opposing ideas and focus on solving problems.

*Real*ationship-Driven Cultures encourage great communication. Our Five Mindsets lay the foundation for how we treat each other. Positive interactions set the stage for great communication. When we are relaxed with and have trust in each other, we can openly communicate, share our thoughts, challenge each other, and passionately disagree while maintaining a good relationship. Purpose creates common goals and work. Together, Mindsets and Purpose create Unity, which provides the motivation and energy to ensure our communications are thorough and focused on searching for the best solutions.

* * *

These six Relational Pillars—trust, respect, mutual benefit, empathy, consistency, and communication—encompass the emotional, practical, and ethical dimensions needed for strong, positive relationships. Proactively creating an environment where our actions encourage these pillars sets the stage for creating a work culture where strong, positive relationships are the norm.

CHAPTER 10

THE PATH FORWARD: TRANSFORMING CULTURES THROUGH *REAL*ATIONSHIPS

How we focus on the human aspect of our organizations matters. If we are not careful, even well-intended efforts can have unintended consequences, creating division rather than unity. Many modern approaches to workplace culture emphasize categorizing individuals based on traits, identities, or working styles. While understanding differences is valuable, an overemphasis on categorization can create silos, reinforce separations, and make collaboration feel transactional rather than relational.

At its core, an organization is a collection of relationships, and relationships thrive when people feel valued as individuals while also recognizing their shared purpose as part of something greater. Instead of focusing on what sets us apart, we should prioritize what brings us together. This is why Fostering Unity and Enriching Self-worth must be intentional and grounded in a framework that strengthens connections, builds trust, and encourages people to support one another. When we see each other first and foremost as fellow humans, we create an environment where people don't just work together, but truly thrive together.

My greatest hope is that you feel inspired to act. Whether your steps are big or small, what matters is the direction: toward a culture where relationships thrive. Building stronger, more connected organizations doesn't happen overnight, but every thoughtful action you take contributes to that transformation. Even the smallest changes, like offering sincere feedback, prioritizing collaboration, or fostering mutual respect, can have an impact.

The beauty of fostering *Real*ationship-Driven Cultures is that everyone plays a role. While companies must lead the charge, individuals are equally responsible for nurturing relationships within their span of influence. Imagine the power of an organization where leadership and employees work in tandem to strengthen relationships and create a shared sense of purpose.

Who Holds the Responsibility?

Organizations Lead the Way

A company sets the tone for how relationships are treated. Policies, culture, and leadership practices determine whether relationships are prioritized or pushed aside in favor of immediate results. Companies must intentionally create systems, environments, and expectations that foster relationships. This includes starting with understanding the importance of relationships as described in the Three Foundational Beliefs presented and aligning their strategies with the principles outlined in this book: Mindsets, Purpose, Involvement, and Service.

Individuals as Relationship Champions

While organizational systems amplify the power of relationships, individuals must take personal ownership. One of the challenges, however, is that working on relationships requires effort, patience, and vulnerability—qualities that can be daunting without the right support. For high-potential employees (HiPos), this becomes even more complicated. HiPos often move rapidly through an organization, leaving little time to build meaningful relationships. Their status as "anointed future leaders" can also discourage managers from addressing behaviors that undermine teamwork or trust out of fear of damaging their careers or reputations.

Additionally, self-serving behavior, often the antithesis of strong relationships, can thrive in environments where political power or fear outweighs accountability. Left unchecked, this behavior erodes trust, stifles collaboration, and weakens the very foundation of an organization's culture. But when even one individual chooses to prioritize connection and mutual benefit, the tide can begin to turn.

Why Relationships Matter

Strong relationships are the foundation of strong organizations. When people feel respected, trusted, and valued, they are more likely to invest their energy and talents into the organization. A culture that prioritizes relationships creates an environment where employees want to contribute, collaborate, and grow. This, in turn, builds stronger organizations that can withstand challenges, innovate more effectively, and achieve sustainable success.

But the impact of *Real*ationship-Driven Cultures doesn't stop at the workplace. Better organizations lead to better lives. Employees who experience meaningful connections at work carry those feelings home. Families benefit. Communities benefit. Over time, organizations with strong cultures contribute not just to economic success but to the well-being of society as a whole.

Transforming Work and the World

When organizations embrace the *Real*ationship principles, they contribute to something greater than quarterly profits. They create environments where people connect and thrive, which in turn Fosters Unity, Enriches Self-worth, and builds Resilience. This is the foundation of lasting change, not just in the workplace but in the world.

How We Help Organizations Transform

At bsh, we use the principles of *Real*ationship-Driven Cultures in everything we do. Whether consulting on small, targeted projects or leading large-scale transformations, we design and implement strategies that strengthen relationships and improve performance.

- **Talent Consulting**: Every consulting engagement incorporates these principles. From leadership development to team interventions and culture transformation, we ensure our work drives stronger connections and healthier environments.

- **Executive Search**: We seek leaders who align with the values of *Realationship*-Driven Cultures. These individuals excel in technical skills and relationship skills including fostering trust, respect, and collaboration.

- **Client Partnerships**: Every interaction with our clients reflects our commitment to the power of relationships. We strive to model the principles we teach, ensuring we live our values. No matter the engagement's size, our goal is to transform culture through the strength of relationships.

A Shared Vision for the Future

Our Vision is simple yet profound: To Foster Unity, Enrich Self-worth, and Build Resilience in organizations, empowering people to thrive through the strength of *Realationships*. We accomplish this through our Mission: Strengthening relationships that transform cultures and drive lasting value by creating environments where people connect, collaborate, and grow together.

We love this work because we believe in its transformative power. Strong relationships are not just a strategy; they are the essence of what makes life and work meaningful. As you take the principles of this book and apply them to your organization, know that you are contributing to a better workplace, a better community, and a better world.

Your Next Step

So, what will you do next? Maybe you'll reflect on how you show up in your own relationships at work. Maybe you'll lead a small change in your team's dynamics. Or maybe you'll decide to partner with us to transform your culture in a meaningful way.

Whatever your next step is, take it. Action, no matter how small, is the beginning of change. The journey toward a *Real*ationship-Driven Culture starts with a single decision and grows with each intentional choice you make.

We're here to help you on this journey, whether through talent consulting, executive search, or simply cheering you on as you take the principles of this book and bring them to life. Let's create workplaces where relationships thrive, cultures transform, and people achieve their fullest potential.

This is your moment to act. Let's build something extraordinary—together.

ENDNOTES

1 Elaine Houston, "The Importance of Positive Relationships in the Workplace," PositivePsychology. com, December 30, 2019, https://positivepsychology.com/ positive-relationships-workplace/.

2 Brian Tayan, "The Wells Fargo Cross-Selling Scandal," The Harvard Law School Forum on Corporate Governance, February 6, 2019, https://corpgov.law.harvard.edu/2019/02/06/ the-wells-fargo-cross-selling-scandal-2/.

3 Amrisha Vaish, Tobias Grossmann, and Amanda Woodward, "Not All Emotions Are Created Equal: The Negativity Bias in Social-Emotional Development.," *Psychological Bulletin* 134, no. 3 (May 2008): 383–403, https://doi.org/10.1037/0033-2909.134.3.383.

4 1. Luis Carretié et al., "Emotion, Attention, and the 'Negativity Bias', Studied through Event-Related Potentials," *International Journal of Psychophysiology* 41, no. 1 (May 2001): 75–85, https://doi.org/10.1016/ s0167-8760(00)00195-1.

5   John T. Cacioppo and Gary G. Berntson, "The
    Affect System," *Current Directions in Psychological
    Science* 8, no. 5 (October 1999): 133–37, https://doi.
    org/10.1111/1467-8721.00031.

6   Vaish, et al.

7   Kenneth A. Norman, Ehren L. Newman, and Greg
    Detre, "A Neural Network Model of Retrieval-Induced
    Forgetting.," *Psychological Review* 114, no. 4 (2007):
    887–953, https://doi.org/10.1037/0033-295x.114.4.887.

8   Jack Zenger and Joseph Folkman, "The Ideal
    Praise-to-Criticism Ratio," Harvard Business
    Review, March 15, 2013, https://hbr.org/2013/03/
    the-ideal-praise-to-criticism.

9   1. "APA Dictionary of Psychology," APA Dictionary of
    Psychology: Confirmation bias, accessed March 5, 2025,
    https://dictionary.apa.org/confirmation-bias.

10 P. C. Wason, "On the Failure to Eliminate Hypotheses
    in a Conceptual Task," *Quarterly Journal of Experimental
    Psychology* 12, no. 3 (July 1960): 129–40, https://doi.
    org/10.1080/17470216008416717.

11 Erin M. Landells and Simon L. Albrecht, "Perceived
    Organizational Politics, Engagement, and Stress: The
    Mediating Influence of Meaningful Work," Frontiers,
    June 26, 2019, https://www.frontiersin.org/journals/
    psychology/articles/10.3389/fpsyg.2019.01612/full.

12 "Company: Search Online Etymology Dictionary,"
    Etymology, accessed January 8, 2025, https://www.
    etymonline.com/search?q=company.

13 John T Cacioppo and Stephanie Cacioppo, "The
    Growing Problem of Loneliness," *The Lancet* 391, no.
    10119 (February 2018): 426, https://doi.org/10.1016/
    s0140-6736(18)30142-9.

14 N. Leigh-Hunt et al., "An Overview of Systematic
    Reviews on the Public Health Consequences of

Social Isolation and Loneliness," *Public Health* 152 (November 2017): 157–71, https://doi.org/10.1016/j. puhe.2017.07.035.

15 Steven W. Cole et al., "Myeloid Differentiation Architecture of Leukocyte Transcriptome Dynamics in Perceived Social Isolation," *Proceedings of the National Academy of Sciences* 112, no. 49 (November 23, 2015): 15142–47, https://doi.org/10.1073/pnas.1514249112.

16 Steven W. Cole et al., "Myeloid Differentiation Architecture of Leukocyte Transcriptome Dynamics in Perceived Social Isolation," *Proceedings of the National Academy of Sciences* 112, no. 49 (November 23, 2015): 15142–47, https://doi.org/10.1073/pnas.1514249112.

17 Amy Novotney, "The Risks of Social Isolation," Monitor on Psychology, May 2019, https://www.apa.org/monitor/2019/05/ce-corner-isolation.

18 Jan West, "The Truth about Job Satisfaction and Friendships at Work," NBRI, accessed January 8, 2025, https://www.nbrii.com/employee-survey-white-papers/the-truth-about-job-satisfaction-and-friendships-at-work/.

19 Juliana Menasce Horowitz and Kim Parker, "How Americans View Their Jobs," Pew Research Center, March 30, 2023, https://www.pewresearch.org/social-trends/2023/03/30/how-americans-view-their-jobs/.

20 Sandy Pentland et al., "Social Networks and Collaborative Problem Solving," IDSS, October 23, 2015, https://idss.mit.edu/vignette/social-networks-and-collaborative-problem-solving/.

21 Achyuta Adhvaryu, Namrata Kala, and Anant Nyshadham, *The Skills to Pay the Bills: Returns to on-the-Job Soft Skills Training*, February 2018, https://doi.org/10.3386/w24313.

22 "Coping with Stress at Work," American Psychological Association, October 22, 2024, https://www.apa.org/topics/healthy-workplaces/work-stress.

23 2024 North American Workplace Fulfillment Gap Index, January 2025, https://assets.ricoh-usa.com/j2jqn9lauv41/9zcQSLJloN7voiaskGynk/b6f1d4bbe57384c83e0891b0995668b7/Ricoh_2024_North_American_Workplace_Fulfillment_Gap_Index_January_2025.pdf.

24 Ewelina Purc and Mariola Laguna, "Personal Values and Innovative Behavior of Employees," *Frontiers in Psychology* 10 (April 18, 2019), https://doi.org/10.3389/fpsyg.2019.00865.

25 Sharon Arieli, Lilach Sagiv, and Sonia Roccas, "Values at Work: The Impact of Personal Values in Organisations," *Applied Psychology* 69, no. 2 (January 22, 2019): 230–75, https://doi.org/10.1111/apps.12181.

26 Julia Lührmann et al., "Personal Values and Their Impact on the Opinion Leadership of Managers and Employees in Internal Communication," *Journal of Public Relations Research*, October 11, 2024, 1–22, https://doi.org/10.1080/1062726x.2024.2409652.

27 Gallup, "Gallup Releases New Findings on the State of the American Workplace," Gallup.com, June 11, 2013, https://news.gallup.com/opinion/gallup/170570/gallup-releases-new-findings-state-american-workplace.aspx.

28 Shelly L. Gable and Courtney L. Gosnell, "The Positive Side of Close Relationships," *Designing Positive Psychology*, January 3, 2011, 265–79, https://doi.org/10.1093/acprof:oso/9780195373585.003.0017.

29 Robin I.M. Dunbar, "The Social Brain Hypothesis," *Evolutionary Anthropology: Issues, News, and Reviews*

6, no. 5 (1998): 178–90, https://doi.org/10.1002/(sici
)1520-6505(1998)6:5<178::aid-evan5>3.3.co;2-p.

30 "Health Effects of Social Isolation and Loneliness,"
Centers for Disease Control and Prevention, May
15, 2024, https://www.cdc.gov/social-connectedness/
risk-factors/index.html.

31 George E. Vaillant, *Triumphs of Experience: The Men of
the Harvard Grant Study* (Cambridge, MA: The Belknap
Press of Harvard University Press, 2012).

32 Julianne Holt-lunstad and Timothy Smith, "Social
Relationships and Mortality Risk: A Meta-Analytic
Review," *SciVee*, July 28, 2010, https://doi.
org/10.4016/19911.01.

33 Horowitz and Parker

34 Korducki

35 Houston

36 Tera Allas and Bill Schaninger, "The Boss
Factor: Making the World a Better Place through
Workplace Relationships," McKinsey & Company,
September 22, 2020, https://www.mckinsey.com/
capabilities/people-and-organizational-performance/
our-insights/the-boss-factor-making-the-worl
d-a-better-place-through-workplace-relationships.

37 Juliana Menasce Horowitz, "How Americans View
Their Jobs," Pew Research Center, March 30, 2023,
https://www.pewresearch.org/social-trends/2023/03/30/
how-americans-view-their-jobs/.

38 Allas and Schaninger.

39 Jocelyn Stange, "8 Manager Tips to Reduce
Employee Stress at Work," Employee Success
Software, November 7, 2019, https://www.
quantumworkplace.com/future-of-work/
manager-tips-reduce-employee-stress-at-work.

40 Kristin Ryba, "6 Factors That Make or Break Working Relationships," Employee Success Software, July 15, 2022, https://www.quantumworkplace.com/future-of-wor k/6-factors-that-make-or-break-relationships-at-work.

41 Deirdre Bardolf and Matthew Sedacca, "25% of Remote Workers Say Their Social Skills Have Declined While Working from Home: Survey," New York Post, December 28, 2024, https://nypost.com/2024/12/28/ business/25-of-remote-workers-social-skills-have-de clined-while-working-from-home-survey/.

42 Sara Korolevich, "Workplace Disconnect: A Survey of Manager vs. Employee Perspectives," Checkr, December 13, 2023, https://checkr.com/resources/articles/ workplace-disconnect-survey-report.

43 Ibid.

44 "Salary Structure Survey Results & Trends in 2023," WorldatWork, June 7, 2023, https://worldatwork.org/about/press-room/ salary-structure-survey-results-trends-in-2023.

45 Robert Half, "Remote Work Statistics and Trends for 2025," Robert Half, February 19, 2025, https:// www.roberthalf.com/us/en/insights/research/ remote-work-statistics-and-trends.

46 Rachel Wells, "The Year in Remote Work-2024's Biggest Shifts," Forbes, November 8, 2024, https:// www.forbes.com/sites/rachelwells/2024/11/08/ the-year-in-remote-work-2024s-biggest-shifts/.

47 Samantha M Keppler and Paul M Leonardi, "Building Relational Confidence in Remote and Hybrid Work Arrangements: Novel Ways to Use Digital Technologies to Foster Knowledge Sharing," *Journal of Computer-Mediated Communication* 28, no. 4 (June 12, 2023), https://doi.org/10.1093/jcmc/zmad020.

48 Jen Wardman, "The Secrets to Creating Meaningful Employee Relationships in Hybrid Work Settings," CareerPoint, June 14, 2022, https://careerpoint.com/blog/hr-trends/the-secrets-to-creating-meaningful-employee-relationships-in-hybrid-work-settings.

49 Ted Kitterman, "How Hybrid and Remote Workplaces Help Employees Find Connection," Great Place To Work®, August 15, 2023, https://www.greatplacetowork.com/resources/blog/build-connection-remote-workers.

50 Wardman

51 Horst Siebert, *Der Kobra-Effekt: Wie Man Irrwege Der Wirtschaftspolitik Vermeidet* (München: Piper, 2003).

52 ibid.

53 Gary P. Latham and Silvia Dello Russo, "The Influence of Organizational Politics on Performance Appraisal," *The Oxford Handbook of Personnel Psychology*, September 2, 2009, 388–410, https://doi.org/10.1093/oxfordhb/9780199234738.003.0017.

54 Joel Schwarz, "UW Researchers Can Predict Newlywed Divorce, Marital Stability with 87 Percent Accuracy," UW News, March 27, 2000, https://www.washington.edu/news/2000/03/27/uw-researchers-can-predict-newlywed-divorce-marital-stability-with-87-percent-accuracy/.

55 John Mordechai Gottman and Nan Silver, *The Seven Principles for Making Marriage Work* (London, UK: Orion Spring, 2023).

56 John Mordechai Gottman and Robert Wayne Levenson, "What Predicts Change in Marital Interaction over Time? A Study of Alternative Models," *Family Process* 38, no. 2 (June 1999): 143–58, https://doi.org/10.1111/j.1545-5300.1999.00143.x.

57 Rob DeSimone, "Improve Work Performance with a Focus on Employee Development," Gallup.com, January 19, 2024, https://www.gallup.com/workplace/269405/high-performance-workplaces-differently.aspx.

58 The state of the American workplace, December 2021, https://bendchamber.org/wp-content/uploads/2021/12/Gallup_State_of_the_American_Workplace_Report.pdf.

59 Doug Flaig, "Council Post: Empowering Innovation: How Leaders Can Cultivate Creativity and Drive Change," Forbes, August 13, 2024, https://www.forbes.com/councils/forbesbusinesscouncil/2024/04/24/empowering-innovation-how-leaders-can-cultivate-creativity-and-drive-change/.

60 Richard E. Boyatzis, Melvin Smith, and Ellen Van Oosten, *Helping People Change: Coaching with Compassion for Lifelong Learning and Growth* (Boston, MA: Harvard Business Review Press, 2019).

61 Stanley Milgram, "Behavioral Study of Obedience.," *The Journal of Abnormal and Social Psychology* 67, no. 4 (October 1963): 371–78, https://doi.org/10.1037/h0040525.

62 Stanley Milgram, *Obedience to Authority: An Experimental View* (New York, NY: Harper Perennial Modern Thought, 2019).

63 Solomon E. Asch, "Studies of Independence and Conformity: I. A Minority of One against a Unanimous Majority.," *Psychological Monographs: General and Applied* 70, no. 9 (1956): 1–70, https://doi.org/10.1037/h0093718.

64 Taylor Lauricella et al., "Network Effects: How to Rebuild Social Capital and Improve Corporate Performance," McKinsey & Company, August 2, 2022, https://www.mckinsey.com/capabilities/people-and-organizational-performance/

our-insights/network-effects-how-to-rebuild-socia
l-capital-and-improve-corporate-performance?utm_
source=chatgpt.com.

65 Houston

66 Caroline Buhl et al., "Community Pharmacy Staff's
Knowledge, Educational Needs, and Barriers Related
to Counseling Cancer Patients and Cancer Survivors in
Denmark," *International Journal of Environmental Research
and Public Health* 20, no. 3 (January 27, 2023): 2287,
https://doi.org/10.3390/ijerph20032287.

67 Miriam Benitez et al., "Harmonious Passion at Work:
Personal Resource for Coping with the Negative
Relationship between Burnout and Intrinsic Job
Satisfaction in Service Employees," *International Journal
of Environmental Research and Public Health* 20, no.
2 (January 5, 2023): 1010, https://doi.org/10.3390/
ijerph20021010.

68 Wang Jiatong et al., "Impact of Passion at Work on
Emotional Exhaustion: Mediating Role of Negative
Emotions," *Current Psychology* 43, no. 36 (August
28, 2024): 29133–42, https://doi.org/10.1007/
s12144-024-06516-1.

69 Rob Cross, Reb Rebele, and Adam Grant, "Collaborative
Overload," Harvard Business Review, March 19, 2024,
https://hbr.org/2016/01/collaborative-overload.

70 Richard E. Boyatzis and Annie McKee, *Resonant
Leadership: Renewing Yourself and Connecting with Others
through Mindfulness, Hope, and Compassion* (Boston, MA:
Harvard Business School Press, 2005).

71 Samer Saab, "Beyond the Horizon: Crafting
Resilience in the 2024 Workplace," HRTech
Cube -, December 15, 2023, https://hrtechcube.
com/2024-workplace-resilience-trends/.

72 Brian O'Connor, "Employee Mental Health: May 2024 En:Insights Forum," Welcome to SHRM, June 19, 2024, https://www.shrm.org/executive-network/insights/employee-mental-health--may-2024-en-insights-forum.

73 Robert D. Putnam, *Bowling Alone: The Collapse and Revival of American Community* (New York, NY: Simon & Schuster, 2020).

74 Tom R. Tyler and Roderick M. Kramer, *Trust in Organizations: Frontiers of Theory and Research* (Thousand Oaks, CA: SAGE Publications, 2001).

75 Amy Edmondson, "Psychological Safety and Learning Behavior in Work Teams," *Administrative Science Quarterly* 44, no. 2 (June 1999): 350–83, https://doi.org/10.2307/2666999.

76 C. M. Anderson and M. M. Martin, "Why Employees Speak to Coworkers and Bosses: Motives, Gender, and Organizational Satisfaction," *Journal of Business Communication* 32, no. 3 (July 1, 1995): 249–65, https://doi.org/10.1177/002194369503200303.

77 Tom R. Tyler and E. Allan Lind, "A Relational Model of Authority in Groups," *Advances in Experimental Social Psychology*, 1992, 115–91, https://doi.org/10.1016/s0065-2601(08)60283-x.

78 Russell Cropanzano and Marie S. Mitchell, "Social Exchange Theory: An Interdisciplinary Review," *Journal of Management* 31, no. 6 (December 2005): 874–900, https://doi.org/10.1177/0149206305279602.

79 Daniel Goleman, *Emotional Intelligence: Why It Can Matter More than IQ* (London, UK: Bloomsbury, 1996).

80 Svetlana Holt and Joan Marques, "Empathy in Leadership: Appropriate or Misplaced? An Empirical Study on a Topic That Is Asking for Attention," *Journal of*

Business Ethics 105, no. 1 (July 2, 2011): 95–105, https://doi.org/10.1007/s10551-011-0951-5.

81   Goleman

82   Niklas Luhmann and Gianfranco Poggi, *Trust and Power: Two Works by Niklas Luhmann* (Ann Arbor, MI: UMI, 2007).

83   John Bowlby, *A Secure Base: Clinical Applications of Attachment Theory* (Hoboken, NJ: Taylor and Francis, 2012).

84   John Mordechai Gottman and Robert Wayne Levenson, "The Timing of Divorce: Predicting When a Couple Will Divorce over a 14-year Period," *Journal of Marriage and Family* 62, no. 3 (August 2000): 737–45, https://doi.org/10.1111/j.1741-3737.2000.00737.x.

85   P. G. Clampitt and C. W. Downs, "Employee Perceptions of the Relationship between Communication and Productivity: A Field Study," *Journal of Business Communication* 30, no. 1 (January 1, 1993): 5–28, https://doi.org/10.1177/002194369303000101.

ACKNOWLEDGMENTS

This book would not exist without the relationships in my life, those who have shaped me, challenged me, encouraged me, and supported me along the way. I am deeply grateful to each of you.

First, to God

For putting the right people in my path, refining my skills and mindsets, and drawing out talents I didn't know I had. For always being with me.

To My Family & Friends

You have been my foundation, my inspiration, and my greatest source of strength.

- **Mom & Dad (Roy & Garnette Miller)** – Thank you for a childhood filled with love. You instilled in me the values of hard work, care for others, the unwavering courage to take on life's challenges, and always believing that God is real and good. Your model of relationships has shaped the way I see the world. Our shared love of racing created many memories and life lessons. We worked very hard but gained many rewards. I look forward to making more memories.

- **My Sisters (Leslie Cantin & Cindy Miller)** – You've shown me that relationships can be different and equally good. I cherish our time growing up and for doing life together as adults. Your constant support and love means the world to me. Your encouragement of my many adventures has been helpful. I look forward to many more years of sharing life.

- **My Wife & Daughter (Sherri & Hannah Miller)** – You are my rocks, my greatest support, and my deepest source of love. Through countless adventures, ups and downs, and all the twists and turns along the way, you have stood by me with unwavering love and encouragement. You allow me to be fully myself, embracing my many ideas, pursuits, and my deep love of work, while always keeping me grounded in what truly matters – relationships. I couldn't do this without you.

- **Terry Graham & Jane Graham** – Thank you for welcoming me into your family with open arms. Terry, though you are no longer with us, your impact remains. Your wisdom and kindness taught me to appreciate life's smaller moments. I will always cherish our shared love of Penn State football. Jane, your warmth and generosity have made me feel truly at home, and I am grateful for the love and support you continue to give.

- **Jodi Graham, Steve Graham & Deb Graham** – From the very beginning, you made me feel like part of the family. The time we've spent together whether sharing stories, laughing, or simply enjoying each other's company has added so much joy to my life. I'm grateful for the good times we've had and look forward to many more.

To My Mentors & Influencers

Your belief in me and your insights on relationships and organizations have shaped my work in profound ways.

- **Ginger Labine** – You taught me how to think critically about organizations, not just in terms of structures and strategies, but in understanding the deeper dynamics that drive success. You helped me see that relationships are at the heart of every thriving workplace. Your insights shaped my perspective on leadership, culture, and human connection.

- **Lesa Litteral** – Your guidance helped me grow not only as a leader but also as a person. You challenged me to see the good in others, to recognize their potential, and to lead with both strength and compassion. Your mentorship shaped the way I approach relationships, leadership, and the impact I strive to have on those around me.

To My Colleagues

The conversations, challenges, and shared experiences have helped shape the ideas in this book.

- **Bob Welsh** – Navigating the transition from corporate life to consulting alongside you has been invaluable. Our deep conversations about organizations continue to challenge and expand my thinking, and I am grateful for the insight and perspective you bring.
- **Chaz Freutel** – Your insights challenged me to see my work not just as a mission to impact people and organizations, but also as a business that needs to thrive financially and advance the Kingdom.
- **Dana Valley** – Your insight helped me clarify and articulate my ideas. You pushed me to communicate the connections between the elements of this model. Your ideas made this work stronger, and I am deeply grateful.
- **Cindy Miller** – Your help with distilling my random thoughts and ideas into graphics helped refine and clarify my messages. Thanks for always asking good questions. Also, thank you for the graphics in this book.

To My Editors & Publishers

You made this book possible by refining my ideas and pushing me to make them better.

- **Kary Oberbrunner** – Your encouragement and belief in this book kept me going through the highs and lows of the writing process. Thanks for your support.

- **Sarah Grandstaff** – Thank you for helping me navigate the publishing process and for being a source of motivation. Your guidance made this book possible.
- **Teri Kojetin**– Thanks for your attention to detail and your willingness to push the project to completion. I appreciate your ideas, advice, and collaboration on the many aspects of creating a book.
- **Jill Ellis** – Your thoughtful feedback pushed me to express exactly what I wanted to say, strengthening this book in ways I couldn't have done alone. I am grateful for your insight and challenge.

To the Researchers & Thought Leaders Who Inspired My Thinking

Your work has profoundly shaped my understanding of relationships and organizational life.

- **Louis Carter** – You helped me see myself, my career, and my work in a new light. Your belief in my talent inspired me, and your perspective on the human side of organizations, especially the power of connection, challenged and deepened my thinking. I am grateful for your insight, encouragement, and the lasting impact you've had on my journey.
- **Dr. Richard Boyatzis** – You taught me the power of positive mindsets and how to inspire others to become their best selves. Your work shaped my understanding of leadership, emotional

intelligence, and the role of relationships in meaningful change. The insights I've gained from you are woven into my approach.

- **Dr. David Cooperrider** – You showed me how to improve organizations through a positive lens, shifting the focus from fixing problems to amplifying strengths. Your work on Appreciative Inquiry and large-scale engagement has been foundational in how I approach change, both in theory and in practice. Your teachings are embedded in my work, shaping the very foundation of this book and my approach to relationships in organizations.

ABOUT THE AUTHOR

Bryan has nearly 30 years of experience in talent management, working internally as head of talent management and as an external consultant. He has worked with small businesses and Fortune 200 companies, including non-profits. Bryan is comfortable with and passionate about working with all levels of the organization. He has successfully worked with the front line through C Suite across all regions, including North America, South America, Europe, the Middle East, and Asia.

Throughout his corporate career, Bryan was responsible for overall talent management. His innovative and collaborative approaches resulted in unique solutions to increase the contribution of individuals and teams. As a leader, Bryan engaged his teams by creating an environment of development, empowerment, collaboration, and shared risk.

Bryan refined his natural talent for creating a vision, developing strategies, and motivating organizations to accomplish the vision throughout his career. Bryan successfully built the talent function for three different organizations, designed and implemented a change function in four organizations, and a project management office in one organization. His collaborative approach creates solutions relevant in context and leverages diverse thoughts and ideas.

Bryan's education includes a BS in Business Administration focused on Management and Marketing from Penn State University and an MS in Positive Organization Development and Change from Case Western Reserve University. He has also completed executive education at Harvard University in Strategic Human Resource Management and MIT in Leading Change in Complex Organizations. Bryan is certified in a wide range of assessments and finds the data valuable in helping individuals and teams improve performance.

When Bryan isn't helping organizations transform, he enjoys spending time with his wife, Sherri, and daughter, Hannah, in Westerville, OH, near Columbus. Having varied interests, he enjoys traveling to new destinations, biking through scenic trails, and writing about relationships, enriching not just his professional life but also his personal life.

BRING THE MESSAGE TO LIFE

Inspire your team with a keynote or workshop that redefines how relationships fuel performance. Practical. Powerful. Unforgettable.

bshTalentSolutions.com

Made in the USA
Middletown, DE
03 April 2025

73627432R00134